THE
COLORADO
PLATEAU

Must-See
Natural and
Cultural
Features

JOHN ANNERINO

FARCOUNTRY
PRESS

In the writing of this book, every effort was made to conform to traditional Native American spelling of names and features based on tribal dictionaries and ethnographies.

ISBN 10: 1-56037-598-1
ISBN 13: 978-1-56037-598-2

© 2014 by Farcountry Press
Photography © 2014 by John Annerino, except where credited otherwise
Text © 2014 by John Annerino

Cover: Hovenweep Castle. PHOTO BY JOHN ANNERINO
Back cover: Dead Horse Point. PHOTO BY JOHN ANNERINO
For photo requests and permissions, contact www.johnannerinophotography.com

For more information about our books, write Farcountry Press,
P.O. Box 5630, Helena, MT 59604; call (800) 821-3874;
or visit www.farcountrypress.com.

Library of Congress Cataloging-in-Publication Data on file.

Created, produced, and designed in the United States.
Printed in the United States.

18   17   16   15   14   1   2   3   4   5   6

TABLE OF CONTENTS

Denver

COLORADO

Rio Grande

Juan NF

Chaco Culture NHP

Bandelier NM

Santa Fe

Petroglyph NM

Albuquerque

El Malpais NM

NEW
MEXICO

ibola NF

N

KEY

National Forest:	NF
National Historical Park:	NHP
National Monument:	NM
National Park:	NP
Navajo Tribal Park:	NTP
State Historic Monument:	SHM
State Park:	SP
Wilderness Area:	WA

THE ESSENTIAL COLORADO PLATEAU

Comprising 140,000 square miles of the Four Corners states of Utah, Arizona, New Mexico, and Colorado, the semi-arid, mile-high physiographic province of the Colorado Plateau ranges in elevation from 2,540 feet at Lava Falls on the Colorado River in Grand Canyon National Park, Arizona, to the 14,000-foot peaks towering over the river's headwaters at 10,184-foot La Poudre Pass in Rocky Mountain National Park, Colorado. The Colorado Plateau is divided into six geographic sections—Grand Canyon, High Plateaus, Uinta Basin, Canyonlands, Navajo, and Datil—and is defined by its spectacular landforms and brilliant stratigraphy that include laccolithic peaks, dissected plateaus, deep canyons and narrows, verdant river valleys, and multi-hued geological marvels of arches, windows, natural bridges, monuments, mesas, hoodoos, and spires. Shaped by wind, water, freeze-thaw erosion, and fault block uplifts, the plateau is drained by the Colorado, Green, San Juan, Little Colorado, Dirty Devil, and Escalante Rivers, and myriad tributaries that traverse a spectrum of life zones from cool alpine forests to blistering Sonoran deserts.

The Grand Staircase

The Colorado Plateau's geology, like no other region in North America, is revealed in a grand staircase and brilliant palette of natural colors offering a variety of outdoor activities:

- **Clarion Formation:** Pink hoodoos, cliffs, and amphitheaters of Bryce Canyon National Park. Activities: Hiking and sightseeing.

- **Dakota Sandstone:** Buff rimrock and potholes of Hovenweep National Monument. Activities: Hiking and sightseeing.

- **Entrada Sandstone:** Salmon-pink and red arches, windows, spires, and stone temples of Arches and Capitol Reef National Parks. Activities: Hiking and sightseeing.

- **Navajo Sandstone:** Vermilion to white arches, cathedrals, domes, narrows, rimrock, and temples of Zion and Canyonlands National Parks and Buckskin Gulch-Paria Canyon Wilderness. Activities: Canyoneering, climbing, hiking, and whitewater rafting.

- **Kayenta Sandstone:** Brown to red cliffs and rimrock of Deadhorse Point State Park. Activities: Climbing, hiking, and sightseeing.

- **Wingate Sandstone:** Red cliffs of Capitol Reef National Park and Newspaper Rock State Historic Monument. Activities: Climbing, hiking, and sightseeing.

- **De Chelly Sandstone:** Reddish arches, alcoves, buttes, cliffs, mesas, and spires of Monument Valley Navajo Tribal Park and Canyon de Chelly National Monument. Activities: Hiking and sightseeing.

- **Cedar Mesa Sandstone:** Tan canyons and rimrocks of Natural Bridges National Monument. Activities: Hiking and sightseeing.

The Grand Canyon

The Grand Canyon, alone, offers its own amazing geological spectrum of colors and activities: Hiking the Grand Canyon from rim-to-river or rim-to-rim, or rafting the Colorado River from Lees Ferry to Diamond Creek, you will pass through each of the colorful geological layers below that span 1.7 billion years.

- **Kaibab Limestone:** Gray to brown rimrock, cliffs, caves, and waterfalls. Activities: Hiking, sightseeing, caving, and river running.

- **Coconino Sandstone:** Buff to gold cliffs, walls, and temples. Activities: Hiking, climbing, sightseeing, and river running.

- **Hermit Shale:** Tan to red rimrock. Activities: Hiking, sightseeing, and river running.
- **Supai Formation:** Red ledges and cliffs. Activities: Hiking, sightseeing, and river running.
- **Redwall Limestone:** Red to salmon-pink caverns, cliffs, and walls. Activities: Hiking, sightseeing, route finding, and river running.
- **Tonto Group:** Red to tan platforms, ledges, and walls. Activities: Hiking, sightseeing, and river running.
- **Vishnu Schist:** Dark gray to black gorges and walls. Activities: Hiking, sightseeing, and river running.

The Grand Circle

Traveling the Grand Circle through the Four Corners region, you will visit modern national parks and monuments, tribal parks, and state parks that celebrate the extraordinary landmarks that abound throughout the Colorado Plateau. But you will also step back in time and have the privilege of seeing and experiencing a cultural legacy that dates back 11,000 years to Archaic hunters and gatherers who roamed the region on a never-ending quest for fire, food, water, and shelter. Ancient peoples who followed their primordial trails and used their temporary camps in this formidable landscape included the Fremont Culture and Ancestral Puebloans, who built great cliff dwellings and painted and carved panels of rock art that left an indelible, if mystifying, record of their travels. Their traditional art, culture, and life ways were emulated by their Pueblo descendants and others who migrated into the region. So, too, you will crisscross and follow the routes and trails of Spanish missionary explorers and conquistadors, mountain men, government surveyors, pioneers, settlers, cowboys, and horse thieves who viewed this land long before the Colorado Plateau's first national monument, El Morro National Monument, New Mexico, was established on December 8, 1906, by President Theodore Roosevelt.

Using This Guide

Each of the chapters in this guide includes an introductory overview of the area's landscape, people, and culture, driving directions, visitor center locations, campground information, scenic drives and points of interest, trailheads and brief trail or route descriptions, and web links.

Delicate Arch. PHOTO BY NEAL HERBERT, NPS

ARCHES NATIONAL PARK

Landscape, People, and Culture

Comprising 76,359 acres of slickrock desert, Arches National Park is a wonderland of stone surrounded by the great Western landscapes of the Green and Colorado Rivers, Manti La Sal Mountains, Dead Horse Point, and Canyonlands. Eons of wind, rain, snow, flash floods, and freeze-thaw erosion sculpted freestanding sandstone arches, fins, spires, and domes found nowhere else on Earth. More than 2,500 arches have been catalogued in this mile-high desert of piñon and juniper that sits atop a 300-million-year-old seabed of salt. Capped by a 300-foot layer of Entrada Sandstone, it faulted and eroded, producing an extraordinary landscape that beckons 750,000 visitors from around the globe each year.

A beautiful yet austere no-man's-land, Arches was roamed seasonally by Archaic peoples, Fremont and Ancestral Puebloans, and Ute. Amid amazing landmarks that offered shelter from the harsh elements, they sought veins of chalcedony and chert to flint-knap tools, scrapers, spears, and, later, arrowheads. Slickrock water pockets brimming with rainwater and snowmelt sustained their desert journeys during

Wolfe Ranch cabin. PHOTO BY NEAL HERBERT, NPS

forays to hunt desert bighorn sheep, mule deer, jackrabbits, and lizards and to gather juniper berries, yucca fruit, and seeds. But they were just passing through, and little remains of their mysterious journeys but lithic scatters, stone shelters, and rock art.

Bypassed by Spanish explorers, government surveyors, and river expeditions, Arches was located in the back of beyond east of Moab, where Mormon pioneers established the Elk Mountain Mission in 1854. But it beckoned Civil War veteran John Wesley Wolfe to homestead the Bar–DX Ranch on Salt Wash from 1888 until 1910. Cowboys later grazed cattle in Arches' sparse grasslands and penned stock in "slickrock corrals." Yet few seemed drawn to the scenery until Hungarian miner Alexander Ringhoffer "discovered" Arches while prospecting the 5,298-foot Klondike Bluffs in 1922. Ringhoffer spread the word and tried to broker a deal with the Denver and Rio Grande Railroad to build a tourist attraction at Klondike Bluffs. The deal fell short, but the genii was out of the bottle. President Herbert Hoover established Arches National Monument on April 12, 1929. Author Edward Abbey bunked in a government trailer and had a literary epiphany while working as a seasonal park ranger in 1956 and 1957. President Lyndon B. Johnson established Arches National Park on January 20, 1969. The rest is history.

DRIVING AND HIKING ACCESS:

From the north: From I-70 20 miles east of Green River, Utah, take Exit 182 and drive 27 miles south on U.S. Highway 191. Turn left at the sign for Arches National Park and drive through the Entrance Station to the Arches Visitor Center. Fill your water bottles with "ancient, naturally filtered" desert groundwater at faucet dispensaries and begin your adventure.

From the south: From South Main Street in downtown Moab, Utah, drive 4.8 miles north on U.S. Highway 191. Turn right at the sign for Arches National Park and drive through the Entrance Station to the Arches Visitor Center.

Arches Scenic Drive:

From the visitor center, the 19-mile-long paved scenic drive leads past the Great Wall through Salt Valley to Devils Garden. Highlighted here are six viewpoints, roadside stops, and hikes in between: Park Avenue, Courthouse Towers, The Windows, Delicate Arch, Fiery Furnace, and Devils Garden.

- **Stop 1: 2.5 miles, Park Avenue Viewpoint.** Formed in the Slickrock Member of Entrada Sandstone, the profile of the ancient Egyptian Queen Nefertiti can be seen overlooking the candlestick spires of the Candelabrum and the 4,982-foot Courthouse Towers. An enjoyable 1-mile walk descends 320 feet in elevation through this miniature Monument Valley to The Organ and the Arches Scenic Drive at Courthouse Towers Viewpoint.

- **Stop 2: 2.8 miles, Manti La Sal Mountains Viewpoint** of 12,721-foot Mount Peale and a summit rim of alpine peaks crowned with snow in winter. The laccolithic peaks were named *La Sierra de la Sal,* "The Mountains of Salt," in 1776 by padres Francisco Atanasio Domínguez and Silvestre Vélez de Escalante.

- **Stop 3: 4.1 miles, Courthouse Towers Viewpoint** of The Organ, the Three Gossips, and 4,537-foot Tower of Babel. In a handwritten March 20, 1854, letter from William W. Handlin to Brigham Young, Handlin wrote from Mexico that the Spanish history of the Indians "says the Indians came from the Tower of Babel." The 1-mile Park Avenue hike ends here.

Hoodoos in Devils Garden. PHOTO BY JOHN ANNERINO

Tower of Babel. PHOTO BY JOHN ANNERINO

■ **Stop 4: 9.5 miles, Balanced Rock pullout.** Teetering 130 feet atop a friable pedestal of the Carmel Formation, Balanced Rock is a literary landmark made famous by author and environmentalist Edward Abbey. During his seasonal patrol work as a park ranger, Abbey lived in a small trailer at the end of a dirt road in the slickrock wilderness that provided inspiration for his book, *Desert Solitaire: A Season in the Wilderness.*

■ **Stop 5: 9.7 miles, The Windows Scenic Drive** turnoff leads 2.7 miles east to The Windows Trailheads. On your way, stop and see the stone goblins in Garden of Eden, 5,653-foot Elephant Butte, and Owl Rock.

The Windows Trailheads. Follow the 1-mile Windows Loop Trail to reach Turret Arch, (64 feet high, 39-foot span), North Window (51 feet high, 93-foot span), and the South Window (66 feet high, 105-foot span), a favorite sunset destination. Across the road, follow the 0.5-mile Double Arch Trail to see blue skies framed by flying buttresses of slickrock Entrada Sandstone (105 feet high, 163-foot by 60-foot spans) that served as a movie location for *Indiana Jones and the Last Crusade.*

Return to Arches Scenic Drive and resume car tour to Devils Garden.

■ **Stop 6: 11.7 miles, Delicate Arch turnoff.** Turn right and drive the paved 1.3-mile road to the Wolfe Ranch parking area and Delicate Arch Trailhead. Delicate Arch Overlook is 1 mile east. The chinked weather-beaten log cabin here was built in 1906 by Civil War veteran John Wesley Wolfe. A rock art panel of Ute petroglyphs of desert bighorn sheep and men on horseback mark the Delicate Arch Trail. (See The Hike: Delicate Arch Trail, page 13.)

Domes in Devils Garden. PHOTO BY JOHN ANNERINO

Balanced Rock. PHOTO BY NEAL HERBERT, NPS

Return to Arches Scenic Drive and resume car tour to Devils Garden.

- **Stop 7: 15.2 miles, Fiery Furnace Viewpoint** and turnoff. Named for the luminescent red hues of its sandstone spires at sunset, the Fiery Furnace can be an oven in mid-summer when temperatures climb above 100 degrees. (See The Exploratory Walk: Fiery Furnace, page 14.)

- **Stop 8: 19 miles, Devils Garden Campground** entrance and loop road. Tucked into the sandstone hollows, nooks, and crannies of Devils Garden, 50 campsites (tent sites to group sites) are available by reservation March 1 through October 31. Phone (877) 444-6777.

- **Stop 9: 19.4 miles, Devils Garden Trailhead.** An easy 1.6-mile round-trip trail pinched between sandstone fins leads to Landscape Arch. The 306-foot-long and 6-foot-thick span of slickrock Entrada Sandstone forms the park's longest and most fragile looking arch.

The Hike: Delicate Arch Trail

This moderate 3-mile round-trip hike climbs 480 vertical feet to Delicate Arch, one of the most rewarding destinations on the Colorado Plateau. The worn footpath up the slickrock of cross-bedded sandstone is pleasing and aesthetic and offers exposed views of Salt Wash, Cache Valley, and Winter Camp Wash. As you approach the high point, you'll walk through a "dugout" in the trail. Stop and look through the window-sized pothole arch above it. Take a seat on the stone ledge used as a bench, sip some "ancient water," and wait for sunset to brush Delicate Arch orange and salmon pink. Forty-five feet tall and 33 feet wide, Delicate Arch is comprised of slickrock Entrada Sandstone

Double O Arch. PHOTO BY NEAL HERBERT, NPS   *Landscape Arch.* PHOTO BY JACOB W. FRANK, NPS

Twilight, Delicate Arch.
PHOTO BY JOHN ANNERINO

supporting a truss of the Curtis Formation. Called "The Chaps" and "Schoolmarms Bloomers" by Moab cowboys in the 1880s, wishbone-shaped Delicate Arch is a Utah icon recognized around the world. (Many visitors use Delicate Arch to frame the distant Manti La Sal Mountains in the background of their photos.) Allow yourself enough time before dark to enjoy the breezy return romp down the slickrock to the trailhead. Spring and fall are best. Summer may prove tough, hot, and crowded.

The Exploratory Walk: Fiery Furnace

In comparison to the open air, slickrock ramble of the Delicate Arch Trail, the Fiery Furnace Walk is a journey of discovery more akin to a subterranean adventure. For spirited and adventure-minded hikers, a 2-mile exploratory "walk" will test—or hone—your scrambling, bouldering, orienteering, canyoneering, and spelunking skills. Thread your way in the semi-darkness between narrow fins and towering spires in look-alike terrain across hanging ledges, slickrock cul-de-sacs, drop-offs, squeeze-throughs, and crawlways to explore Skull Arch, Walk-Through Arch, and Surprise Arch. Looming 55 feet overhead, Surprise Arch's 63-foot span was first seen by park rangers in 1963. Fiery Furnace has proved disorienting and difficult for many lost visitors unaccustomed to what park brochures describe as "a maze-like labyrinth of narrow sandstone canyons." So permits are required and ranger-led walks are advised. If you venture alone or with companions, take mental pictures on your way into the stone maze so you can safely return along the same route.

 ADA Accessible:

Visitor center and restrooms
Balanced Rock Viewpoint
Lower Delicate Arch Viewpoint
Devils Garden restrooms
Devils Garden Campground (Site #4H)
Park Avenue Viewpoint
Wolfe Ranch cabin and rock art

Fiery Furnace. PHOTO BY JACOB W. FRANK, NPS

Dead Horse Point. PHOTO BY JOHN ANNERINO

DEAD HORSE POINT STATE PARK

Landscape, People, and Culture

Comprising 5,362 acres of classic Colorado Plateau lands, Dead Horse Point State Park is bookmarked between the freestanding roseate landmarks of Arches and the soaring Island in the Sky of Canyonlands National Park. Rimmed by sheer cliffs 2,000 feet above the Colorado River, Dead Horse Point's colorful layer-cake geology dates from the 195-million-year-old rimrock of Kayenta Sandstone that visitors perch atop to the 306-million-year-old Honaker Trail Formation that Colorado River rafters paddle through. Thrust in the midst of immense canyon country that appears three dimensional at first light, 5,680-foot Dead Horse Point offers one of the most dramatic views in North America. For that reason, the state park was established in 1959 to preserve its "incredible panoramic views."

This precipitous and arid plateau was home to Archaic peoples, contemporaneously Ancestral Puebloans and Fremont, and Ute. Rimrock potholes on Dead Horse Point and Mesa offered humans and wildlife ephemeral water during summer monsoons and spring snowmelt. Desert bighorn sheep, deer, and rabbits were hunted on Dead Horse Point and roasted on fires fed by juniper tree tinder. The trees also provided bark for making sandals, cordage, and sleeping mats. Juniper berries, among a host of other plants, supplemented Ancestral Puebloans' and Fremont people's plots of corn, beans, and squash before they vanished from the area around AD 1300.

Spanish explorers, government surveyors, trappers, Mormon colonists, and Colorado and Green River expeditioners were on their way to somewhere else. Some stayed to put down roots. Among the first was wagon master Norman Taylor. He came west from Ohio with Brigham Young's original colony in 1847, leading 14 wagons of pioneers, supplies, and livestock to start ranching in Moab. Taylor's cattle and horses ranged west on Arth's Pasture and Gray's Pasture near Dead Horse Point, where oil, uranium, potash, and tourism later boomed. Hollywood, too, discovered what one scientist wrote in 1859 was the "wildest and most fantastic scenery to be found on the surface of the globe." Rivaling Monument Valley 150 miles south, canyon country provided the scenic locations for dozens of major movie productions, from John Ford's *Wagon Master* to Walter Hill's *Geronimo, An American Legend*. No location offered a more dramatic setting than Dead Horse Point, a principal costar in scenes from *Thelma and Louise, Mission Impossible II,* and *The Lone Ranger.* Come see for yourself.

Dead Horse Point Scenic Drive

From the visitor center, the 1.4-mile paved scenic drive leads past viewpoints, roadside picnic stops, and trailheads to Dead Horse Point.

DRIVING AND HIKING ACCESS:

From the north: From I-70 about 20 miles east of Green River, Utah, take Exit 182 and drive 19.2 miles south on U.S. Highway 191. Turn right at the sign for Utah Highway 313, Dead Horse Mesa Scenic Byway, and drive 14.6 miles to the Dead Horse Point State Park turnoff. Turn left to stay on UT 313 and drive 4 miles to the entrance station. It's 2.2 miles farther to the visitor center.

From the south: From South Main Street in downtown Moab, Utah, drive 11.2 miles north on U.S. Highway 191. Turn left at the sign for Utah Highway 313, Dead Horse Mesa Scenic Byway, and drive 14.6 miles to the Dead Horse Point State Park turnoff. Turn left to stay on UT 313 and drive 4 miles to the entrance station. It's 2.2 miles farther to the visitor center.

- **Stop 1: 0.2 mile, Kayenta Campground entrance** and loop road. Located on the western edge of Dead Horse Mesa, 21 campsites (sheltered ramadas and tables, charcoal grills, restrooms, and 1 handicap site) are available by reservation. (Moenkopi Group Site offers 1 group space for 30 people, a pavilion and restrooms; located between the entrance station and visitor center). For reservations phone (800) 322-3770.

Trails and Viewpoints

Kayenta Campground, the visitor center, and Dead Horse Point offer easy rim access to overlooks via hiking and mountain bike trails (some paved).

Hiking

1.5-mile Big Horn Overlook Trail   0.25-mile Nature Trail (paved)
0.5-mile Colorado Overlook Trail   0.5-mile Dead Horse Point (paved)
0.5-mile East Rim Trail   2.5-mile West Rim Trail

Hiking and Mountain Biking

1.1-mile Intrepid Loop   4.2-mile Great Pyramid Overlook Trail
9.0-mile Big Chief Overlook Trail

Colorado River bends from Dead Horse Point. PHOTO BY JOHN ANNERINO

Timbers of old corral, legend of Dead Horse. PHOTO BY JOHN ANNERINO

- **Stop 2: 1.1 miles, The Neck. Dead Horse Point corral.** Pull out on the right (west) side of the road and cross the road to see the rustic remains of what the author was told was the Dead Horse Point corral. It fenced off the 30-yard-wide Neck that penned mustangs on Dead Horse Point until cowboys could drive them to market.

- **Stop 3: 1.4 miles Dead Horse Point.**
  The Legend. If you can somehow ignore the scenery, you can still find the potholes on the edge of Dead Horse Point that begat the legend. There are many variations. One that gleams with authenticity was told by Aunt Lydia Taylor Skewes and recounted in the 1972 book, *Grand Memories*, by The Daughters of the Utah Pioneers. In 1881, Aunt Lydia recounted the simple facts. There was a drought. The Taylors drove their cattle to summer pasture. When the rain finally came, it filled the potholes. The shallow holes dried up. The horses climbed into the deep potholes to drink but

couldn't get out. They starved. When the Taylors returned in the fall, the potholes were filled with dead horses.

The View. From the edge of the rimrock, you can take in the great sweep of canyon country from the Gooseneck of the Colorado River south to the 11,360-foot Abajo Peak in the Abajo Mountains on the distant horizon. Between here and there, Archaic peoples stalked desert bighorn sheep with spear-throwing atlatls thousands of years earlier. A mysterious fur trapper named Denis Julien carved his sunburst inscription "D. Julien 1836" while running the Green and Colorado Rivers in a makeshift bull-hide boat; wildcat drillers floated a wooden oil rig 20 miles down the Colorado River to drill for oil in the Cane Creek aniticline in 1924; Thelma and Louise drove a 1966 blue Thunderbird convertible off Fossil Point into the "Grand Canyon" (the real Grand Canyon is 300 miles to the south); and IMF agent Ethan Hunt dared the impossible by solo jumping and climbing Dead Horse Point without a rope during his vacation.

 ADA Accessible:

Visitor center and restrooms
Kayenta Campground
   and restrooms
Nature Trail (paved)
Dead Horse Point:
   shaded pavilion, picnic
   areas, and restrooms

Globemallow.
PHOTO BY JACOB W. FRANK, NPS

Hoodoos, Big Spring Canyon. PHOTO BY JOHN ANNERINO

CANYONLANDS NATIONAL PARK

ISLAND IN THE SKY
Landscape, People, and Culture

Comprising 337,598 acres of lofty plateaus and soaring mesas cut by deep tributary chasms, Canyonlands National Park's daunting landscapes form what remains the most remote, rugged, and unexplored wilderness in the contiguous United States. Roaring beneath the 11,000- to 12,000-foot laccolithic peaks and subalpine forests of the Henry, Manti La Sal, and Abajo Mountains, the Green and Colorado Rivers cut though colorful sedimentary rock formations of the Colorado Plateau during an uplift 15 million years ago, creating three distinct landforms divided by the ancient rivers that shaped them. The semi-arid 6,240-foot-high plateau of Island in the Sky looms a vertical 0.5 mile above the sandstone labyrinths and rock art panels of the Maze to the southwest, and the grabens, canyons, and minarets of the Needles to the southeast. Called a "wilderness of rocks" by government surveyors, Utah's largest national park was established by President Lyndon B. Johnson on September 12, 1964.

Archaic peoples roamed Canyonlands' precipitous slickrock on a tireless quest

White Rim. PHOTO BY JOHN ANNERINO

for food, water, and shelter. They inhabited cliff dwellings hidden in caves and alcoves overlooking terraces that were home to the desert bighorn sheep they hunted. Their ancient trails from the rim tops led down through sheer cliffs to the Green and Colorado Rivers where they fished for squawfish and bass with nets, bone hooks, and hand lines. Ancestral Puebloans and Fremont people, and later the Ute and Paiute, used the same rim-to-river trails to hunt and gather; grow and harvest corn, beans, and squash; and fish. Sometimes wading at low water, other times floating and paddling on driftwood logs, they crossed primeval rivers that Major John Wesley Powell and his men later navigated in 1869 through Labyrinth, Stillwater, and Cataract Canyons.

Pioneer stockmen like John Shafer traced the same trails, forging dizzying switchbacks through sheer walls of Navajo Sandstone to the White Rim to graze cattle, where wildcat oil men drilled for "black gold" during the 1920s, uranium miners explored for "yellow cake" during the 1950s, and rock climbers mantled atop untrod summits during the 1960s and 1970s. These were the same spectacular trails and colorful timelines that created the fabric of

DRIVING AND HIKING ACCESS:

From the north: From I-70 about 20 miles east of Green River, Utah, take Exit 182 and drive 19.2 miles south on U.S. Highway 191. Turn right onto Utah Highway 313, Dead Horse Mesa Scenic Byway, and drive 14.6 miles to the Dead Horse Point State Park turnoff. Continue straight on Island in the Sky Road and drive 6.8 miles to the Canyonlands National Park Visitor Center.

From the south: From South Main Street in downtown Moab, Utah, drive 11.2 miles north on U.S. Highway 191. Turn left at the sign for Utah Highway 313, Dead Horse Mesa Scenic Byway, and drive 14.6 miles to the Dead Horse Point State Park turnoff. Continue straight on Island in the Sky Road and drive 6.8 miles to the Canyonlands National Park Visitor Center.

Canyonlands' remarkable story that visitors and adventurers still seek in its chasms, rivers, and mesas of stone and light.

Island in the Sky Scenic Drive

From the visitor center, the 12.3-mile paved scenic drive leads along the east rim of Island in the Sky past viewpoints, picnic stops, and trailheads to Grand View Point Overlook.

- **Stop 1: 0.2 mile, Shafer Canyon Overlook.** The canyon is named for cattlemen John "Sog" and Frank Shafer, brothers who dynamited a cattle track along an Indian route that lead from the edge of nearby Gray's Pasture down to the White Rim in 1914. It became known as Shafer Trail to uranium miners driving to the Lathrop Canyon Mine in the 1950s.

  Shafer Trail. A spectacular half-day introduction to the White Rim Trail is the 10.2-mile round-trip high-clearance drive down the hairpin, hair-raising Shafer Switchbacks that drop 1,400-feet through Jurassic-aged Navajo Sandstone to the Shafer Camp junction and turnaround. (The Shafer Trail turnoff is located 1 mile east of the visitor center).

  White Rim Trail. The serpentine 100-mile White Rim Trail crosses sandstone benches and terraces, then loops in and around bays and amphitheaters between the lofty rims of Island in the Sky and the gorges of the Green and Colorado Rivers. Cliffs, towers, arches, and scenic camps lure mountain bikers, motocross riders, and 4WD enthusiasts on a one- to three-day inner canyon adventure that traces the hanging ledges of White Rim Sandstone

White Rim Road biking. PHOTO BY NEAL HERBERT, NPS

Rimrock, Island in the Sky. PHOTO BY JOHN ANNERINO

to the Gooseneck Overlook, Musselman Arch, Monument Basin, and the canyon country beyond.

■ **Stop 2: 6.3 miles, Mesa Arch Loop Trail.** The sandy 0.5-mile Mesa Arch Loop Trail climbs 100 feet and leads to 6,800-foot Mesa Arch, Island in the Sky's most popular and photographed destination. Seen in the distance through the 50-foot-wide crevice of this Navajo Sandstone pothole arch are landmark pinnacles that form Islet in the Sky. Highest among them is the Wingate Sandstone and Kayenta caprock spire of 5,835-foot Monster Tower, first climbed by the late, legendary American climber Layton Kor and his partners Cub Shafer and Larry Dalke on December 26, 1963.

■ **Stop 3: 6.5 miles, Grand View Point, Willow Flat Campground, Upheaval Dome junction.** Turn left (south) to continue on the Island in the Sky Scenic Drive.

Upheaval Dome Scenic Drive Detours. From the Island in the Sky Visitor Center, the 4.5-mile paved scenic drive begins at the Grand View Point junction and leads west past viewpoints, picnic areas, and trailheads to Upheaval Dome.

Detour A. 0.2 mile, Willow Flat Campground turnoff. Drive 1 mile south to the campground entrance and loop road. Twelve campsites are available on a first-come, first-served basis (shaded picnic tables, grills, tent sites, and vault restrooms).

Detour B. Green River Overlook. Located 0.25 mile south of Willow Flat Campground, Green River Overlook offers panoramic views in clear skies of the White Rim in Soda Springs Basin, flat-topped 6,227-foot Ekker Butte, the Orange Cliffs, and 11,522-foot Mount Ellen in the Henry Mountains.

Detour C. 0.7 mile, Aztec Butte Trailhead. The sandy 2-mile round-trip hike leads to the foot of 6,312-foot Aztec Butte and climbs 225 feet up and around the slickrock to an Ancestral Puebloan storage granary hidden in an alcove overlooking the depths of Taylor Canyon and the scalloped ridges of Horsethief Point.

Return to Island in the Sky Scenic Drive.

■ **Stop 4: 7.6 miles, Candlestick Tower Overlook.** The 5,865-foot-high Candlestick Tower was first climbed by Jim Dunn and three other climbers in March 1974. To reach the start of the climb, the first ascensionists had to rappel 400 feet down the west rim of Island in the Sky and trudge 2 miles with heavy packs to the base of the 450-foot-tall Wingate Sandstone tower.

Pothole Point, Needles District. PHOTO BY NEAL HERBERT, NPS

■ **Stop 5: 12.3 miles, Grand View Point Overlook and Trail.** A 2-mile round-trip slickrock walk leads to the southern point of Island in the Sky plateau. From the 6,080-foot overlook you can see the sheer wall meanders, goosenecks, and bowknot bends that form the confluence of the Green and Colorado Rivers. Together, they created the dangerous rapids in Cataract Canyon that Major John Wesley Powell faced 4 miles below the confluence. On July 19, 1869, the one-armed Powell climbed from the confluence to view the rugged landscape his expedition was attempting to navigate. "Wherever we look there is but a wilderness of rocks," Powell wrote, "deep gorges where the rivers are lost below cliffs and towers and pinnacles, and ten thousand strangely carved forms in every direction."

THE NEEDLES
Landscape, People, and Culture

Located in one of the most remote corners of the Colorado Plateau, the Needles takes its name from magnificent red and white Cedar Mesa and Cutler Sandstone spires that resemble flaming torches under the glow of sunrise and

DRIVING AND HIKING ACCESS:

From South Main Street in downtown Moab, Utah: Drive 39.4 miles south on U.S. Highway 191. Turn right at the signed exit for Utah Highway 211 and drive the Indian Creek Scenic Byway 34 miles to the Needles Visitor Center in Canyonlands National Park.

sunset. Explored by Captain John Macomb during the San Juan Exploring Expedition in 1859, the Needles were described by expedition geologist John S. Newberry as "a forest of Gothic Spires." It was the same country of which Macomb exclaimed, "I cannot conceive of a more worthless and impracticable region than the one we now found ourselves in."

Drawn to this "worthless" sandstone desert of pinnacles, arches, and canyons that offered scant water and little pasturage were pioneers, cowboys, prospectors, and outlaws who scratched out a living with pluck, fortitude, and six-guns. West of the Needles in what was called "the wildest and most remote country in the West," native Utahn Joseph C. Biddlecome pioneered Robbers Roost Ranch in 1908, the haunt of outlaws Butch Cassidy, the Sundance Kid, and the Wild Bunch. Biddlecome carved a sign at Roost Spring to keep other bandits at bay that read, "BEWARE 14 notches on my gun J. B." East of the Needles from 1914 to 1975, the Scorup-Sommerville Cattle Company ran beeves from the Dugout Ranch along Indian Creek beneath towering cottonwood trees and landmarks inspired by the West's fastest guns, North Six-shooter and South Six-shooter Peaks. During the 1950s, Arches National Park Superintendent Bates Wilson and backcountry guide Kent Frost were enamored with the country and pushed for Canyonlands to be established as a national park. They got their wish in 1964. Come see what the fuss was all about.

Hands pictographs, Cave Springs. PHOTO BY JOHN ANNERINO

Indian Creek Scenic Byway points of interest en route include Home of Truth homestead, Abajo Mountains and 11,360-foot Abajo Peak, Indian Creek Canyon, Newspaper Rock State Historic Monument (see pages 33-35), Indian Creek BLM rock climbing area, North and South Six-shooter Peaks, historic Dugout Ranch (owned by The Nature

Conservancy), and a Canyonlands outpost (gas, groceries, campsites, and charter flights).

Needles Scenic Drive

From the visitor center, the 6.4-mile paved scenic drive leads past viewpoints, roadside stops, and hikes before ending at the Big Spring Canyon Overlook.

- **Stop 1: 0.3 mile, Roadside Ruin.** A 0.5-mile round-trip loop hike leads to a fragile and well-preserved Ancestral Puebloan storage granary.

- **Stop 2: 2.4 miles, Salt Creek and Cave Springs turnoff.**

  Cave Springs Loop Trail. The enjoyable 0.6-mile Cave Springs Loop Trail leads to the Cave Springs Cowboy Camp, recognized on the National Register of Historic Places for its cultural importance. From 1891 until 1975, Cave Springs was used by cattleman John Albert Scorup and cowboys who bunked in the Needles, a day's ride from ranch headquarters, to graze and water the herds they protected from rustlers. They survived on black coffee, Dutch oven sourdough biscuits, bacon, beans, and "sonuvabitch" stew. Outside the cave, rare colorful Ancestral Puebloan pictographs of handprints and a bird adorn the Cedar Mesa Sandstone walls above a seep springs, indicating this was a reliable water source for cowboys and Native Americans for 1,000 years. At the end of your visit, two wooden ladders help you climb up the scenic slickrock and return to the trailhead.

- **Stop 3: 2.8 miles, Squaw Flat Campground and Elephant Hill turnoff.** Squaw Flat Campgrounds A and B offer 26 campsite sites (picnic tables, fire grills, tent pads, and restrooms) nestled beneath ledges and hummocks of Cedar Mesa Sandstone on a first-come, first-served basis.

Colorado River. PHOTO BY USBLM MOAB FIELD OFFICE   *Under the rim dwelling.* PHOTO BY USBLM

Chesler Park. PHOTO BY NEAL HERBERT, NPS

Elephant Hill Trailhead is the gateway to Chesler Park. A 6-mile round-trip hike leads to the Chesler Park overlook of the Needles, and a 10.8-mile round-trip hike leads to the amazing double-windowed Druid Arch.

- **Stop 4: 5.6 miles, Big Spring Canyon Overlook.** Short roadside trails lead to great picnic spots on the slickrock and sunset views of hoodoos and Big Spring Canyon. An 11-mile round-trip hike from road's end leads to the Confluence Overlook 1,000 feet above the Green and Colorado Rivers and views of the 30-square-mile sandstone puzzle of the Maze.

River Trips

Commercial Trips. There are few better ways to savor the remote beauty of Canyonlands National Park than a two- to four-day oar- or paddle-powered river trip down the Colorado River through Cataract Canyon, or a four-day river trip down the Green River through Desolation Canyon. For a list of Canyonlands National Park's sanctioned river guides and outfitters, visit www.utah-adventures.com/destination.cfm?id=1237824454208 or www.nps.gov/cany/planyourvisit/guidedtrips.htm.

Private Trips. If you want to taste the adventure of early river runners like fur trapper Denis Julien in 1836, explorer John Wesley Powell in 1869, and kayaker-swimmer Harold H. Leich in 1933, few journeys will stir your soul more than a private river trip down the West's greatest river through Canyonlands National Park to the head of Lake Powell in Glen Canyon National Recreation Area. A popular launch site for the four- to six-day, 95-mile river trip is Potash, 15 miles southwest of Moab, Utah. Between this put-in on the Colorado River at Mile 48.7 on river left and the take-out at Hite Marina at Mile 169, you'll float through the neck-craning goosenecks and wild beauty of Dead Horse Point, Lathrop Canyon, and The Loop to Spanish Bottom at the head of Cataract Canyon.

Tranquil camps and beautiful hikes along the way include Horsethief Canyon camp at Mile 26 on river left; Indian Creek Ruins hike at Mile 16.5 on river left; The Loop camp at Mile 6.5 on river right; passage through the confluence of the Green and Colorado Rivers at Mile 0 (from this point, river miles start with Mile 216 and count down); and Spanish Bottom camp and the Dolls Hike to the Maze at Mile 213 on river right.

Once you enter Cataract Canyon, you're on the "river of no return" until you run—or swim—the legendary rapids of Cataract Canyon like Brown Betty, North Seas, Mile Long, and the Big Drops of Kolb, Satan's Gut, and Little Niagara Rapids. During peak spring runoff you'll encounter the biggest, most exciting water in the continental United States, a ride you'll never forget. Below the Big Drops, a good camp (depending on water level) is below what used to be Rapid 25 at Mile 202.7 on river right. A motorized tow out across 30 miles of Lake Powell's still waters to Hite Marina can be reserved and often picks up private river trips in the bay of Gypsum Canyon at Mile 196.5 on river left. Private permits and nominal fees are required. For complete details, visit Canyonlands National Park's excellent river running site, www.nps.gov/cany/planyourvisit/rivers.htm.

Big Drop Three. PHOTO BY NEAL HERBERT, NPS

Newspaper Rock. PHOTO BY JOHN ANNERINO

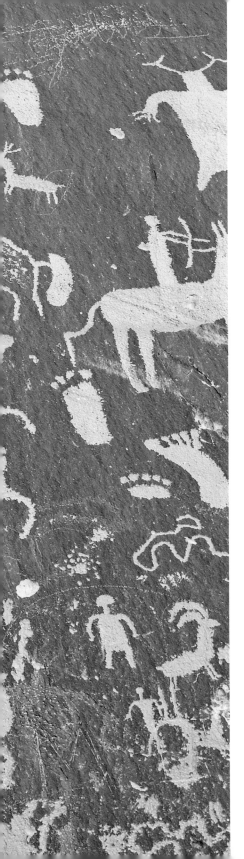

NEWSPAPER ROCK STATE HISTORIC MONUMENT

Landscape, People, and Culture

Tucked away in Shay Canyon along the verdant course of Indian Creek, Newspaper Rock is a 200-square-foot panel of Wingate Sandstone perched at the foot of a 6,804-foot dome of Kayenta and Navajo Sandstones. Made with hammerstones and chisels, and later with metal tools, 650 petroglyphs have been carved, pecked, and scraped into the manganese-iron desert varnish, exposing the lighter Wingate Sandstone beneath the dark veneer.

Dating back 2,000 years from 100 BC to AD 1540 and later, the remarkable petroglyphs were the work of Archaic peoples, Ancestral Puebloans, and Fremont, Ute, Navajo, and Euro-American explorers. To the Navajo, or Diné, who also lived and hunted in the area, it's known as *Tsé Ha Ne,* "The Rock That Tells the Story." Recognized as the West's most impressive, best preserved rock art site, Newspaper Rock is listed on the National Register of Historic Places. It's location on the cottonwood tree-lined Indian Creek and its symbols indicate Newspaper Rock was a signpost

Handprint art.
PHOTO BY JACOB W. FRANK, NPS

on an established travel corridor used by ancient hunters and traders. The route led from the forested 11,000-foot Abajo Mountains all the way through Indian Creek Canyon to its confluence with the Colorado River (Mile 16.5), where these people inhabited cliff dwellings, used storage granaries, and pecked and painted petroglyphs and pictographs. En route to and from their seasonal homes amid the desert cliffs and chasms above the confluence of the Green and Colorado Rivers, they hunted deer, elk, bear, and desert bighorn sheep with atlatls, and later with bows and arrows. They cooked and ate the bounty of meat, sun-dried and jerked the remains, scraped and tanned the hides, and revered the spirit animals that blessed them. Hand-shaped pieces of deer and elk antlers, and bighorn sheep horns, were used to flint-knap chalcedony and chert into spear and arrow points, knives and hide scrapers, and hammerstones and chisels. The latter were used to shape mano and metate grinding stones, and to chisel hunting stories, visions, and spirit beings into the stone canvas of Newspaper Rock.

DRIVING AND HIKING ACCESS:

From the north: From South Main Street in downtown Moab, Utah, drive 39.4 miles south on U.S. Highway 191. Turn right at Utah Highway 211 and drive the Indian Creek Scenic Byway 12.3 miles to Newspaper Rock State Historic Monument.

From the south: From North Main Street in downtown Monticello, drive 14.3 miles north on U.S. Highway 191. Turn left onto Utah Highway 211 and drive the Indian Creek Scenic Byway 12.3 miles to Newspaper Rock State Historic Monument.

Indian Creek Scenic Byway points of interest en route include Home of Truth homestead, the Abajo Mountains, and Indian Creek Canyon.

The View. A short paved hiking path leads from the parking area to the foot of Newspaper Rock. Take your time to study the profusion of amazing and mysterious symbols: handprints; normal and six-toed footprints; animal tracks and paw prints of bears, bear cubs, and badgers; deer, elk, and desert bighorn sheep, both standing alone and walking in herds; lone bison; men on horseback shooting elk and deer with bows and arrows; tanned animal hides; human figures, horned men, and horned lizard shamans; snakes, watercourses, and trails (perhaps the route through Indian Creek Canyon to the Colorado River); and spoked wheels, concentric circles, spirals, encircled crosses, and a cemetery cross.

♿ ADA Accessible:

Visitor center and restrooms

Newspaper Rock art. PHOTO BY JOHN ANNERINO

Horse Collar Ruins. PHOTO BY JACOB W. FRANK

NATURAL BRIDGES NATIONAL MONUMENT

Landscape, People, and Culture

Comprising 7,636 acres of piñon- and juniper-covered slickrock canyons, rimrock, and serpentine meanders of the 6,500-foot-high Cedar Mesa, Natural Bridges is located at road's end on the southwestern flanks of the 11,000-foot Abajo Mountains. Tucked between Elk Ridge, the Goosenecks of the San Juan River, and the Red Rock Plateau, it is drained by spectacular chasms and shallow interlaced tributaries that lured first peoples and early visitors to seek out three monumental natural bridges spanning the meandering creeks of White and Armstrong Canyons. The bridges were formed between 164 million and 10,000 years ago, as floodwaters scoured, eroded, and cut new passages through porous walls of Permian-aged Cedar Mesa Sandstone. Among these is Sipapu Bridge, the second-largest natural bridge in the world (bested by Rainbow Bridge at 309 feet high and 278 feet long; see page 59).

Here Archaic and Fremont peoples and Ancestral Puebloans hunted, gathered, fished, and tilled crops in the red rock canyons, mesas, and deserts stretching south from Canyonlands to the San Juan River and beyond. Ute, Paiute, Navajo, and Hopi ancestors later migrated into the area and followed ancient trails among cliff dwellings and bridges through hallowed terrain adorned with sacred shrines, ceremonial kivas, and color pictographs of red bears, water glyphs, handprints, dinosaurs, and shield-carrying warriors.

All three natural bridges have been named and renamed by a string of explorers. In 1883, a Paiute guide named Joe led prospector Cass Hite from his mining camp at Dandy Crossing on the Colorado River at the head of Glen Canyon into White Canyon, what the Paiute called *Ma-Vah-Tak-Tusip*, "Under the Horse's Belly." To the legendary Utah explorer's delight, Hite found ". . . copper streaks . . . Moqui [Hopi] houses," and three large stone bridges he named President, Senator, and Congressman.

Under the hand of John Albert Scorup, the Scorup-Sommerville Cattle Company grazed 7,000 to 10,000 head of cattle on 1.8 million acres south from the Dugout Ranch in Canyonlands all the way to Natural Bridges. In 1903, Scorup's brother James guided mining engineer Horace J. Long on horseback, outfitted with a week's provisions, camera gear, and survey equipment, along precipitous cliffs in and out of box canyons, finally reaching Armstrong Canyon and the bridge they named Little Bridge (Hite's Congressman Bridge). Long named the largest bridge after his wife, Augusta, and the middle bridge after James Scorup's mother, Carolyn.

An account of Scorup and Long's expedition, written by gold miner and avid geologist W. W. Dyar, was published in the 1904 edition of *The Century Magazine*. With Harry Fenn's dramatic drawings based on Long's photographs, the article, "The Colossal Bridges of Utah; A Recent Discovery of Natural Wonder," garnered attention far and wide. In 1906, the Salt Lake City painter Henry Lavender Adolphus Culmer ventured into the isolated canyons. On August 16, he sketched Augusta Bridge (now Sipapu Bridge), what he described as "a most magnificent and shapely structure." Culmer's oil on canvas painting of Augusta Bridge became one of three coveted landscape paintings

DRIVING AND HIKING ACCESS:

From Blanding, Utah: Drive 3.9 miles south on U.S. Highway 191 to the signed turnoff for Utah Highway 95. Turn right onto UT 95, the Bicentennial Highway, and drive 30.2 miles to UT 275. Turn right and follow UT 275, Natural Bridge Drive, 10.1 miles to the Natural Bridges National Monument Visitor Center.

he made of Natural Bridges that were bought by expedition leader Colonel Edwin F. Holmes and later published in the March 1907 issue of *National Geographic*. The resulting exposure led President Theodore Roosevelt to establish Natural Bridges National Monument—Utah's first national monument—on April 16, 1908. While mapping the park, William B. Douglass, a surveyor with the General Land Office, gave the bridges the Hopi names we use today.

Natural Bridges Campground and Bridge View Drive loop road. Nestled in the piñon and juniper, the campground offers 13 sites (tent sites, grills, picnic tables, and pit toilets). A sign warns campers not to approach chipmunks and mice due to an outbreak in 2006 of bubonic plague. Don't feed the rodents!

Astronomers. Natural Bridge's remoteness from civilization unveils the darkest night skies measured by the National Park Service's Night Sky Team. The monument was the first Dark-Sky Park certified by the International Dark-Sky Association. Come camp under these magnificent stars and see your shadow cast by starshine.

Bridge View Drive. From the visitor center, the one-way, 9-mile paved scenic drive loops counterclockwise atop Cedar Mesa past well-signed overlooks, trailheads, and a picnic area, and returns to Natural Bridges Campground and Visitor Center. The distances below are from the junction where the loop starts and ends.

- **Stop 1:** 2.0 miles, picnic area on left.
- **Stop 2:** 2.3 miles, Sipapu Bridge Trailhead on right. The 1.2 mile round-trip trail into White Canyon descends and climbs 500 vertical feet each way on stone-cut steps, aided by metal hand railings, and three wooden ladders to see the 220-foot-high, 53-foot-thick, 268-foot-long span of Sipapu

Rock art, Natural Bridges. PHOTO BY JACOB W. FRANK, NPS

Bridge. Derived from the Hopi words *Sípàapuni*, "hatchway where the Hopi emerged to the Fourth world," and *Sipápuni*, "Place of Emergence," the actual sacred spot is located far to the south in northern Arizona's 3,000-foot-deep Little Colorado Gorge. Halfway down the Sipapu Bridge Trail, stop at the Bridge Overlook, look across the canyon, and try to pick out two small Ancestral Puebloan dwellings high atop the cliff walls.

■ **Stop 3: 2.6 miles, Horse Collar Ruins Overlook and Trailhead on right.** The 0.6-mile level round-trip trail leads to the edge of the rimrock overlooking White Canyon and Horse Collar Ruins. Rediscovered in 1936 by Natural Bridges National Monument's first curator, Ezekiel "Zeke" Johnson, Horse Collar Ruins is a descriptive name for the wood and leather harness appearance of the oval twin entrances of the Ancestral Puebloan storage granaries adjoined by a ceremonial kiva.

■ **Stop 4: 4.5 miles, Kachina Bridge Trailhead on right.** The 1.4-mile round-trip trail into White Canyon descends and climbs 400 vertical feet each way to see the 210-foot-high, 93-foot-thick, 203.25-foot-long span Kachina Bridge. The name is derived from the Hopi word *Katsina*, "Spirit Being," believed to dwell atop Kachina Peaks (12,000-foot San Francisco Mountains) in northern Arizona, what the Hopi revere as *Navatekiaoui*, "Place of Snow on the Very Top." The word Kachina was used to describe the panel of color pictograph handprints on the circular Ancestral Puebloan dwelling near the bridge, which includes white figures of shamans or dancers.

■ **Stop 5: 6.4 miles, Owachomo Bridge Trailhead on right.** The 0.4-mile round-trip trail into Armstrong Canyon descends and climbs 180 vertical

Sipapu Bridge. PHOTO BY JACOB W. FRANK, NPS   *Horse Collar Ruins.* PHOTO BY NEAL HERBERT, NPS

feet each way to see the 106-foot-high, 9-foot-thick, 180-foot-long span. Owachomo is reportedly derived from the Hopi word for "rock mound." The bridge was also known for a time as Edwin Bridge, so named by the Salt Lake Commercial Club. A 1907 black-and-white photograph shows 22 cowboys on horseback riding across the fragile bridge.

 ADA Accessible:

Visitor center and restrooms
Picnic area (one table)
Sipapu Bridge Overlook
Owachomo Bridge Overlook

Fragile Stones: In June 1947, vandals used a jeep and logging chain to pull down a fragile 164-million-year-old landmark, a Cedar Mesa Sandstone hoodoo called the Goblet of Venus on the road to Natural Bridges National Monument. More recently, in 2013, two men pushed over a 170-million-year-old Entrada Sandstone hoodoo in Goblin Valley State Park, Utah. Such vandalism is punishable by fines and jail time.

Zeke Johnson with Goblet of Venus.
PHOTO BY GEORGE GRANT, NPS HISTORIC
PHOTOGRAPH COLLECTION

Kachina Bridge. PHOTO BY JACOB W. FRANK, NPS

Milky Way at Owachomo Bridge. PHOTO BY JACOB W. FRANK, NPS

Hovenweep Castle. PHOTO BY JOHN ANNERINO

HOVENWEEP NATIONAL MONUMENT

Landscape, People, and Culture

Hidden in the vast sweep of the Great Sage Plain between the landmark Sleeping Ute Mountains that rise to nearly 10,000 feet and the ancestral waters of the San Juan River is 6,760-foot-high Cajon Mesa. Archaic peoples roamed the high desert of piñon, Utah juniper, narrowleaf yucca, and snakeweed, hunting mule deer, antelope, and jackrabbits. They sought shelter from summer heat and the cold wind, rain, and snow that blew in from the Southern Rockies, sleeping in animal skins around cook fires beneath canyon ledges and caves. In this parched landscape they collected rainwater and snowmelt from rimrock potholes and canyonhead springs that seeped through the Dakota Sandstone near their shelters in the Burro Canyon shale. Ancestral Puebloans survived much the same way, but they developed proficient use of bows and arrows for hunting, and they grew corn, beans, and squash on terraced hillsides in rich soils carried by winds from Monument Valley and the San Juan River 10,000 years earlier. Between AD 1200 and 1300, Ancestral Puebloans built fortified dwellings for 300 people atop the same canyon rims and house-sized boulders that spear-carrying Archaic peoples once survived beneath. But their stone dwellings, ceremonial kivas, and storage granaries were like no others in the American Southwest. They built impregnable masonry towers that were used as lookouts for enemies, as well as for celestial and solar observations.

Leading a hardy contingent of Mormon scouts, guides, and explorers driving five ox-drawn wagons down the south fork of the Spanish Trail, William Dressler Huntington first saw Hovenweep in 1854 during a dangerous cross-canyon expedition to trade with the Navajo for church leader Brigham Young. "Upon seeing the ruins . . ." historian Phil Fauver wrote, "Some in the expedition felt that they had found remnants of the Gadianton Robbers," a secret, ancient group mentioned in the *Book of Mormon*. Twenty years later, Hayden Expedition surveyor Captain John Moss guided photographer William Henry Jackson from Mesa Verde across the desert Utes called *Hovenweep*, or "Deserted Valley," to explore and photograph ruins said to be the homes of "sun worshipers." Word spread slowly, and in 1917 the Smithsonian Institution sent Massachusetts-born anthropologist Jesse Walter Fewkes to conduct an archaeological survey of six ancient villages and castellated towers, which he named and recommended for national monument designation. Recognizing Hovenweep's unique architecture and the "finest prehistoric masonry in the United States," President Warren G. Harding established Hovenweep National Monument on March 2, 1923.

DRIVING AND HIKING ACCESS:

From Blanding, Utah: Drive 14.9 miles south on U.S. Highway 191 to the signed turnoff for Utah Highway 262. Turn left onto UT 262, also known as Trail of the Ancients, and drive east 8.4 miles to the Hatch Trading Post Road and the sign for Hovenweep. Turn left and drive 16 miles east-southeast to Hovenweep Road, County Road 413. Turn left and drive north 6 miles on the Hovenweep Road to the national monument turnoff on the right. Turn right and drive 0.7 mile to the Hovenweep National Monument Visitor Center. This route is paved; dirt roads in the area may be impassable when wet.

From Cortez, Colorado: Drive south 3 miles on U.S. Highway 160/491 and turn right onto McElmo Canyon Road/County Road G. Drive west 30.8 miles and turn right at the sign for Hovenweep onto Belitso Road. Drive 4.4 miles north and west and turn right onto Hovenweep Road, County Road 413. Drive north 6 miles to the turnoff for the national monument on the right. Turn right and drive 0.7 mile to the Hovenweep National Monument Visitor Center.

Square Tower Ruins Campground and loop road. Located 0.25 mile from the visitor center, the campground offers sunrise and sunset views of Sleeping Ute Mountain, with 31 campsites, (shaded tables, grills, tent sites, and restrooms) on a first-come, first-served basis.

Square Tower Trail Loop Hike. From the visitor center, this enjoyable 2-mile rim walk atop Dakota Sandstone slickrock offers easy access to view the largest concentration of pueblos, cliff houses, castles, towers or "Great Houses," granaries, and ceremonial kivas in the monument.

■ **Canyon Overlook Trail.** A short paved trail from the visitor center leads to the edge of Little Ruin Canyon. When archaeologist J. W. Fewkes surveyed the area in 1917, he called it Square Tower Canyon and noted in his report, *Prehistoric Villages, Castles, and Towers of Southwestern Colorado,* that the ruins "were marvelously well preserved."

In a counterclockwise direction you can view:

■ **Tower Point.** A 0.5-mile loop hike off the Square Tower Trail offers what Fewkes called a "commanding view" from the North Fork of Little Ruin Canyon across the 100-foot-deep canyon to Twin Towers and Rim Rock House.

Detail of Square Tower. PHOTO BY JOHN ANNERINO

- **Hovenweep Castle.** Constructed from natural and hand-shaped stones and adobe mortar, Hovenweep Castle was a multi-storied, twin-towered dwelling that included nine adjacent rooms, two kivas, and a defensive doorway that opened toward the canyon rim. Archaeologists speculate that the towers and castles were built for astronomical and solar observations for planting seasonal crops; food storage; and for defense of Hovenweep's precious water supply at Square Tower, Cajon, and Hackberry Springs and other seeps, potholes, and catch basins that were used for drinking, cooking, and crops.

- **Square Tower, viewed from the rim.** (Little Ruin Canyon is closed to visitors.) In his six-part 1892 series "In Search of a Lost Race" for the New York City newsweekly, *Illustrated American,* Smithsonian Institution contract archeologist Warren K. Moorehead wrote that the four-story Square Tower was the "tallest building standing" and was convinced it was used as a defense to protect Square Tower Spring.

- **Hovenweep House.** Once the largest dwelling on the canyon rim, Hovenweep House is perched at the head of the South Fork of Little Ruin Canyon and displays the remains of a rectangular pueblo, multi-chambered semicircular D-shaped tower, and kiva.

- **Rim Rock House.** Some speculate that the narrow holes in the walls of this two-story house were used for warm weather ventilation or as peepholes to keep a lookout for strangers.

- **Eroded Boulder House,** viewed from the rim. (Little Ruin Canyon is closed to visitors.) Originally called Hollow Boulder, two-room Eroded Boulder

Solstice panel. PHOTO BY ANDREW KUHN, NPS

Collared lizard. PHOTO BY NEAL HERBERT, NPS

Stronghold House. PHOTO BY NEAL HERBERT, NPS

House is one of Hovenweep's most unique dwellings because it was constructed inside an 18-by-8-foot, cave-walled boulder chamber. When Fewkes visited this dwelling, he noted the impressions of corncobs that Ancestral Puebloans used to mortar the adobe between the masonry stones.

■ **Stronghold House and Tower.** Formerly called Gibraltar House by the eminent American archaeologist Alfred Vincent Kidder and Mayanist scholar Sylvanus Griswold Morley in 1906, the scenic fortress-like dwelling was precariously built atop a sloping boulder once linked to an inaccessible Dakota Sandstone outcrop by a long, log catwalk.

 ADA Accessible:

Visitor center and restrooms
Canyon Overlook Trail
Campground restrooms
Picnic area (one table)

Outlying dwellings located within the boundaries of the Navajo Nation, Utah

- **Cajon Ruins.** From the visitor center, drive 6.4 miles on the Hovenweep Road to the Cajon Road. Turn right and drive 0.4 mile to the turnoff on the left and follow the 2.8-mile dirt road to Cajon Ruins.

Outlying dwellings located within the boundaries of Canyons of the Ancients National Monument, Colorado

- **Holly Ruins.** Located at the head of Keeley Canyon are Holly House, Holly Tower, Tilted Tower, and a solar shrine. A moderate 4-mile one-way hike leads from Square Tower Campground to the Holly House Trailhead. Walk 1 mile farther and you can access the turnoff for the Horseshoe-Hackberry Ruins Trailhead.

- **Horseshoe House, Horseshoe Tower, and Hackberry Ruins.**

- **Cutthroat Ruins, Cutthroat Castle, and Cutthroat Tower.**

Driving: For current map handouts, online pdfs, and precise driving directions to the turnoffs, and road conditions of the high-clearance 2WD and 4WD dirt roads, check in at the visitor center or visit www.nps.gov/hove/index.htm.

Holly Group. PHOTO BY JACOB W. FRANK, NPS

Cutthroat Castle. PHOTO BY ANDREW KUHN, NPS

Canyons of the Ancients National Monument

Located north of Hovenweep National Monument, the 164,000-acre Canyons of the Ancients National Monument was established under the Antiquities Act by President William J. Clinton on June 9, 2000, because it contains "the highest known density of archaeological sites in the Nation." Revered by the Hopi, Acoma Pueblo, and Laguna Pueblo people, the 20-room Painted Hand Pueblo is called *K'amagashe,* or "White Hands," and is exemplary of the dwellings throughout the monument. The towers, used as lookouts for enemies and for celestial observations, were called *Tuwalanki* by Hopi elders.

Directions: Located 8.5 miles north of Hovenweep Visitor Center, the easy-to-miss turnoff is marked by a wooden macaw bird sign. An unimproved dirt road (impassable when wet) leads 1 mile south to the unmarked trailhead. For up-to-date map handouts, online pdfs, and precise driving directions to the turnoff, and road conditions of the high-clearance 2WD dirt road, visit www.co.blm.gov/ahc.

West and East Mitten Buttes. PHOTO BY JOHN ANNERINO

MONUMENT VALLEY NAVAJO TRIBAL PARK

Landscape, People, and Culture

Comprising 91,696 acres of cloud-hugging mesas, towering spires, purple sage, and terracotta sands, Monument Valley is one of the most sublime and iconic landscapes on Earth. Sweeping east from the 10,328-foot laccolithic dome of Navajo Mountain, Monument Valley's spectacular landmarks soar above the mile-high *Desierto Pintado*, or "Painted Desert." The mythic landscape is known among the Navajo as *Tsé bii' Ndzisgaii*, "Clearings Among the Rocks," and many of its brilliant De Chelly Sandstone sentinels bare holy names rooted in Navajo spiritual beliefs linked to ceremonial traditions and the Four Sacred Mountains of Navajoland, *Dinétah*, "the land." Cliff dwellings, mysterious hand pictographs where shamans "crossed over" to the spirit world, and rock carvings of the Hopi Kachina *Kókopilau*, "Humpbacked Flute Player," offer mute testimony that this extraordinary landscape was revered long before the arrival of the *Diné*, Navajo "people," in AD 1200. Archaic peoples left their marks on the valley's hallowed red stones, as did the *Hisat.sinom*, or "People Who Lived Long Ago," ancestors of the Hopi.

Living in fire-warmed hogans beneath sandstone pinnacles that resembled deities, the Navajo were attacked by Spaniards, kidnapped by slave traders, and marched at gunpoint under the scorched-earth dictum of Colonel Christopher "Kit" Carson. They valiantly resisted at every turn, but 9,000 Navajo could not escape the tortuous Long Walk to Bosque Redondo. Hundreds perished. *Hashkéniinii*, "giving out anger," was not among them, and no leader was said to be more feared than the 35-year-old Navajo chief. During a desperate bid to escape Carson's ruthless troops under the cover of darkness in 1863, Hashkéniinii led 17 family members 50 miles across the rugged high desert to the hidden canyons encircling Navajo Mountain, a sacred peak revered for its protection as *Naatsis'áán*, "Head of the Earth." Sheltered from the bitter wind and snow in fork-poled hogans covered with juniper bark, Hashkéniinii and the Navajo Mountain Diné survived that first cruel winter on slim rations of seeds and pine nuts they collected, tending a small flock of 20 sheep they guarded with their lives. Come spring, they built their flock and herd by round-ing up wild cattle and abandoned sheep that provided meat for food and wool they weaved into clothing and blankets with deer bone awls. Six years later, Hashkéniinii and his people moved to Monument Valley, homeland of the San Juan Paiute and Southern Ute, and shared their bounty with Navajos who survived Carson's merciless campaign. The freed prisoners in turn showed

DRIVING AND HIKING ACCESS:

From the north: From Main Street (U.S. Highway 191) in Bluff, Utah, drive 4.2 miles south on U.S. 191 to the junction with U.S. Highway 163. Continue west and south 41 miles on U.S. 163 to Monument Valley Junction. To reach the historic Goulding's Trad-ing Post Museum, turn right and follow the signs 1.8 miles west. To reach the Monument Valley Navajo Tribal Park Visitor Center and Scenic Road, turn left and drive 3.8 miles to the ranger station, where the drive begins.

From the south: From the junction of U.S. Highways 160 and 163 in Kayenta, Arizona, go north on U.S. 163 and drive 23.6 miles to the Monument Valley Junction, Utah. To reach the historic Goulding's Trading Post Museum, turn left and follow the signs 1.8 miles west. To reach the Monument Valley Navajo Tribal Park Visitor Center and Scenic Road, turn right and drive 3.8 miles to the ranger station, where the drive begins.

Hashkéniinii how to fashion silver he'd discovered into ornaments the Navajo wore, traded, and became famous for. Until his death in 1909, "the last chief of the Navajos" protected Monument Valley from all outsiders.

Hashkéniinii made an exception for John Wetherill. After feasting on rabbits and sweetened coffee with Hashkéniinii and his son Hashkéniinii Begay, Wetherill was given permission to open the Oljato Trading Post. Yet, in spite of the notoriety Wetherill received for aiding Byron Cummings and William B. Douglass in the "discovery" of Rainbow Bridge in 1909, Oljato, which means "moon water," was a bust. And in 1910 the Wetherills moved to Kayenta. It wasn't until Harry Goulding and his wife, Leone, opened Goulding's Trading Post in 1924 that a remote oasis in Monument Valley proved it could thrive. Its success was due in part to the fact that Goulding drove to Hollywood with pictures he insisted John Ford see after hearing a 1938 news report that the director was looking for a Western location to film *Stagecoach*, starring John Wayne. The rest is history. Come see the legendary landscape as immortalized in myth and celluloid.

Monument Valley Scenic Road. From the visitor center, follow the 17-mile dirt loop road through Monument Valley.

- **Stop 1: 0.4 mile, Mitten Buttes vista on left.** The most iconic landmarks in the American West stand before you. Left to right they are 5,597-foot West Mitten Butte and 5,594-foot East Mitten Butte. Called *'Álá Tsoh*, "Big Hands," in Navajo for their resemblance to two bear paws, West and East Mitten Buttes were used as the backdrop for the 1946 John Ford movie, *My Darling Clementine*, starring Henry Fonda as Wyatt Earp.

Merrick Butte and the Lost Silver Lode. Seen from the same vista south of East Mitten Butte is 6,076-foot Merrick Butte. In 1879, Utah prospector Ernest Mitchell and his partner James Merritt (mistakenly

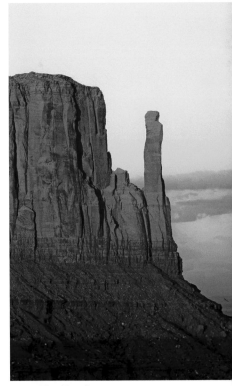

West Mitten Butte, sunset. PHOTO BY JOHN ANNERINO

called Merrick) were shot by "renegades" at the foot of Merrick Butte while leading four mules loaded with silver that assayed 90 percent pure. Mitchell staggered away and died of starvation at the foot of nearby 6,575-foot Mitchell Mesa that now bears his name. Based on a tip from a Navajo scout named Boy With Many Horses, Utah pioneer Henry L. "Old Man" Mitchell launched a search party to recover the bodies of his son and partner for a proper burial. To this day, the mysterious murders remain at the heart of Monument Valley's legendary lost silver mine that may have been Hashkéniinii's secret diggings.

- **Stop 2: 1.1 miles, Elephant Butte vista on left.** The geology and stratigraphy of 5,928-foot Elephant Butte is characteristic of Monument Valley's spectacular De Chelly Sandstone landmarks that sit atop a base of Permian-aged Organ Rock shale capped by the Triassic-aged Moenkopi Formation.

- **Stop 3: 2.9 miles, Three Sisters vista on right.** Rivaling the incredible beauty of the Totem Pole and Yéi Becheii Spires, the 5,722-foot Three Sisters crown the southern arm of Mitchell Mesa. Called *Haashch'eeh diné*, "Holy People," in Navajo for holy people turned to stone, Three Sisters served

Three Sisters. PHOTO BY JOHN ANNERINO

as the backdrop for the 1939 John Ford movie *Stagecoach*, starring John Wayne. The 600-foot-tall South Sister, 325-foot-tall Middle Sister, and 575-foot-tall North Sister were first climbed in 1980-81 by legendary Arizona climber Stan "Bandito" Mish and partners. Rock climbing is no longer permitted in Monument Valley, unless you're Clint Eastwood (see the Totem Pole entry below).

■ **Stop 4: 3.7 miles, John Ford Point Junction.** Turn right and drive 0.4 mile to the parking area beneath Three Sisters. John Ford Point is the rocky promontory 100 yards south, where visitors can have their pictures taken sitting in a saddle atop a Navajo horse. The 1956 John Ford movie, *The Searchers*, starring John Wayne as Ethan Edward, filmed a pivotal scene on the point. Among the 10 movies Ford made in Monument Valley, *The Searchers* was recognized by the American Film Institute in 2008 as the greatest Western in America's 10 greatest film genres. Director Gore Verbinski returned to the same spot to film Johnny Depp and Arnie Hammer surveying the country from their horses in the 2013 Disney movie, *The Lone Ranger*.

Return to the scenic road and resume car tour.

■ **Stop 5: 5.0 miles, Hub Junction.** Turn left and drive the sandy track 1 mile through the narrow valley beneath the beautiful walls of 5,932-foot Rain God Mesa (left) and 5,525-foot Thunderbird Mesa to Totem Pole Junction.

■ **Stop 6: 6.0 miles, Totem Pole Junction.** Turn right and drive 0.9 mile to Sand Springs vista. From the overlook, you can see the perennial course of Sand Springs Wash and the sweep of dunes stretching to the foot of the 5,621-foot Totem Pole and 5,325-foot Yéi Becheii Spires.

Totem Pole. PHOTO BY JOHN ANNERINO   *Yéi Becheii Spires.* PHOTO BY JOHN ANNERINO

Totem Pole. Called *Tsé Ts'óózi*, "Slim Rock," in Navajo for its resemblance to a talking prayer stick used by medicine men, the Totem Pole was used as a location for the 1975 Clint Eastwood movie, *The Eiger Sanction*, starring Clint Eastwood and costar George Kennedy. In the action-adventure film, Eastwood, playing Jonathan Hemlock, and Kennedy, playing his trainer Ben Bowman, "climbed" the tallest and thinnest spire in North America as training for a daring ascent of Switzerland's notorious North Face of the Eiger.

Yéi Becheii Spires. Called *Yéi Becheii*, "Grand Father of the Yé'ii," in Navajo, the supernatural spirits pray and dance in the healing ceremony of *Klédze Hatál*, "Night Chant."

Return to the scenic road and resume car tour.

- **Stop 7: 7.6 miles, Artist's Point Junction.** Turn right and drive 0.3 mile to Artist's Point vista. Towering overhead is the flinty point of 5,988-foot Spear Head Mesa. Far below, you can see Gypsum Creek Wash threading the pass between Merrick Butte and East Mitten Butte.

Return to the scenic road and resume car tour.

- **Stop 8: 9.3 miles, North Window Junction.** Turn right and drive 0.5 mile through the pass between 5,614-foot Camel Butte (left) and 5,794-foot Cly Butte to the North Window parking area. Starring James Stewart, Gregory Peck, and John Wayne playing General William Tecumseh Sherman, the epic 1962 movie, *How the West Was Won*, included scenes of horse-drawn immigrant wagons using the scenic pass.

Return to the scenic road and resume car tour.

- **Stop 9: 10.3 miles, Scenic Road junction.** Turn right and drive 3.5 miles back to the visitor center.

Scenic Tours: For guided scenic tours of Monument Valley and Mystery Valley, visit Monument Valley Tours: navajonationparks.org/htm/monumentvalley-tours.htm. For custom photographic and scenic tours of Monument Valley, Hunts Mesa, Mystery Valley, and secret arches, visit Crawley's Monument Valley Tours: www.crawleytours.com/tour/page3.htm.

Hiking: Wildcat Trail. This trail is the only hike you can do in the Navajo tribal park without a tribal guide. The enjoyable, self-guided 3.2-mile loop trail leads through the purple sage around the base of West Mitten Butte. The trailhead is at the parking area north of the visitor center. Carry water. Allow 1.5 to 2 hours.

Ear of the Wind Arch. PHOTO BY JOHN ANNERINO

Rainbow Bridge. PHOTO BY NPS

RAINBOW BRIDGE NATIONAL MONUMENT

Landscape, People, and Culture

Cradled between the forested heights of 10,328-foot Navajo Mountain and the serpentine confluence of the Colorado and San Juan Rivers, Rainbow Bridge was once lost in the rugged maze of cliffs, canyons, and badlands of the Rainbow Plateau. Formed more than 200 million years ago, the parabolic Navajo Sandstone arch rests atop a base of Kayenta Sandstone and forms a natural, desert varnish–streaked bow across Bridge Creek. Spanning 278 feet and towering 309 feet over the streambed, Rainbow Bridge is the largest natural bridge in the world. From the time of ancestral Paiute, Ute, Hopi, and Navajo, Rainbow Bridge was a sight to behold and pray to, and it is still deeply revered by their descendants today. An ancient shrine at the foot of this great bridge dating back 1,500 years set precedence for Navajo medicine men called *ha'athali*, "singers," to chant the Blessingway and Protectionway healing ceremonies beneath the sacred span of *Tsé naa Na'ni'ahi*, "Rock Arch," commonly known as *Nonnezoshi*, "Rainbow Turned to

Stone." Navajo medicine man Floyd Laughter told historian Karl W. Luckert "the Rainbow was left for prayer and offerings to the power of the Holy People."

No outsider was said to know of its existence until Navajo elder Blind Salt Clansman (*Áshiihí bin áá' ádiní*) shared the secret with Oljato Trading Post owners John and Louisa Wetherill in 1907. From that moment, the race was on to "discover" Rainbow Bridge. Outfitted and led by John Wetherill with Paiute guides Nasja Begay and Mike's Boy, professor Byron Cummings, surveyor William B. Douglass, and their party followed on horseback through stands of piñon and juniper, threading slickrock canyons for four-and-a-half saddle weary days into the rugged depths of Bridge Canyon to Rainbow Bridge. On August 14, 1909, they triumphantly claimed discovery of the bridge that had been seen years earlier by prospectors W. F. Williams and his father J. Patterson Williams. In 1884 the Williamses were led to Rainbow Bridge by Navajo chief and medicine man Hashkéniinii. W. F. Williams later recounted: "There were names cut on the base of the free end of the arch of Rainbow Bridge when we saw it." The inscriptions included little-known figures Billy Ross, Jim Black, George Emmerson, Ed Randolph, Wydell, and Montgomery.

More famous men joined that list and penned colorful accounts of their memorable adventures through Navajo Mountain's labyrinth of sandstone canyons, including novelist Zane Grey and President Theodore Roosevelt. In 1913 they were both guided to Rainbow Bridge on separate expeditions led by John Wetherill and Nasja Begay. In his wonderful book of Western travels, *A Book Lover's Holiday in the Open*, Roosevelt wrote of his August 13, 1913, visit: "The arch is the sign of the rainbow, the sign of the sun's course over the earth, and to the Navajo it is sacred. This great natural bridge, so recently 'discovered' by white men, has for ages been known to the Indians . . . almost under it there is what appears to be the ruin of a very ancient shrine."

Three years earlier, President William Howard Taft established Rainbow Bridge National Monument on May 30, 1910. The monument comprises 160 acres in the upper reaches of Forbidding Canyon, a tributary of Glen Canyon

DRIVING AND HIKING ACCESS:

From Page, Arizona: Drive 43 miles southeast on Arizona Highway 98 to the Inscription House turnoff. Turn left and drive 13.4 miles north on Navajo 16 until you reach the Navajo Mountain turnoff. Turn left onto the dirt road and drive 18.6 miles to the Navajo Mountain junction. Turn left onto road 161 and drive 5.8 miles to park at the historic Rainbow Lodge site.

(now Lake Powell). Go see the Rainbow Bridge for yourself, by foot, horseback, or boat.

Rainbow Lodge Ruins. In 1923, brothers S. I. and Hubert Richardson built the lodge beneath the crags of Navajo Mountain as an investment to provide tourist accommodations and access through Cliff Canyon to Rainbow Bridge National Monument. Ownership changed hands several times, and in 1946 Arizona Senator Barry M. Goldwater bought the lodge, but it burned down in 1951.

The Rainbow Trail. This extraordinary journey loops around the southwest flanks of Navajo Mountain and follows the paths of Native American medicine men, pilgrims, cowboys, sheepherders, and Anglo explorers, prospectors, surveyors, novelists, and ex-presidents. In spite of its lore and beauty, it is a remote and rugged trail that requires preparation, conditioning, and orienteering skills. There is no cell service. If you need communication, lease a satellite phone. But don't expect the authorities to scramble a helicopter if you sprain an ankle; you're on your own. Spring and fall are the best seasons to

Rainbow Bridge Trail. PHOTO BY NPS

Claret cup cactus. PHOTO BY JACOB W. FRANK, NPS

embark on this spellbinding trek. Summer heat and storms, with lightning and flash foods, and winter cold, wind, ice, and snow can be unforgiving.

From the Rainbow Lodge site at 6,400 feet above sea level, the undeveloped Rainbow Trail is 13 miles one way. It has an elevation loss and gain of 2,500 vertical feet in each direction. Cache food and water on the trek in and return by the same trail. Or prearrange a vehicle shuttle at the Cha Canyon Trailhead 8.5 miles west of Navajo Mountain Trading Post. The author circumnavigated Navajo Mountain via the 1922 Wetherill-Bernheimer Expedition route, tracing the "South Trail" through Cliff Canyon and returning on the 12.5-mile "North Trail" (Hashkéniinii's route) to Owl Bridge in Cha Canyon before veering over the summit of Navajo Mountain and War God Spring, and back down to the Navajo Mountain Trading Post.

Scenic Mileposts, Camps, and Water. Stay attentive for the steel pipe mileposts and cairns that mark the trail.

Mile 1. 6,200 feet, hike through piñon and juniper and cross First Canyon.

Mile 2. 6,200 feet, cross the deep drainage of Horse Canyon.

Mile 3. Milepost.

Mile 5. 6,400 feet, Yabut Pass (or "Sunset Pass"). This undeveloped rest stop and camp in the piñon and juniper beneath beautiful sandstone domes and spires offers spectacular views of Navajo Mountain, Cummings Mesa, and Glen Canyon. From this high point, the rocky trail plummets 1,600 vertical feet in 2 miles to the bottom of Cliff Canyon.

Mile 7. 4,800 feet, Cliff Canyon. Follow the boulder-strewn streambed beneath towering walls of Navajo Sandstone 1 mile to First Water.

Mile 8. First Water campsites and good seasonal water.

Mile 9. Redbud Pass junction. If you keep your eyes peeled, you'll see pictographs and the rustic remains of a ceremonial forked-pole cedarwood Navajo hogan. Turn right and follow the narrow sandy trail between sheer walls and climb about 200 vertical feet to Redbud Pass.

Mile 9.4. Redbud Pass. Scramble down the other side through the narrow slot blasted by the Wetherill-Bernheimer Expedition in 1922, marking the occasion with their inscription.

Mile 10. Redbud Creek confluence, veer left.

Mile 10.6. Milepost.

Mile 10.9. Bridge Creek and Navajo Mountain Trading Post Trail junction. Turn left and follow Bridge Creek downstream to Second Water Campsite. Seasonal water.

Mile 12. Bridge Creek and gate, close gate.

Mile 12.8. Echo Camp. A former horsepack camp, the perennial springs, rusty bed springs, and overhanging alcove offer summer shade and winter shelter and make this a great campsite near the end of your journey.

Mile 13. 3,900 feet, Rainbow Bridge. Do not climb on Rainbow Bridge.

Hiking Permits Required
Navajo Nation Parks & Recreation
navajonationparks.org/permits.htm

Topographical Maps Needed: U.S. Geological Survey 7.5-minute maps: Chaiyahi Flat, Arizona, Rainbow Bridge, Utah-Arizona.

Road Map Suggested: AAA Indian Country Guide Map
www.amazon.com/Map-AAA-Guide-Indian-Country/dp/B005MZ53RI

Navajo Guided Horse Pack Trips
Rainbow Bridge Outfitters
P.O. Box 310075
Mexican Hat, Utah 84531

Navajo Country Guided Trail Rides
www.a-aa.com/trailride/

Rainbow Bridge Boat Tours
www.lakepowell.com/play/tours/boat-tours/rainbow-bridge-.aspx

Balanced Rock. PHOTO BY JOHN ANNERINO

GLEN CANYON NATIONAL RECREATION AREA

Landscape, People, and Culture

Seen from the windy summit of 10,328-foot Navajo Mountain on the Utah-Arizona border, Glen Canyon glimmers with the blue light of Lake Powell and stretches more than 186 miles from the confluence of the Dirty Devil and Colorado Rivers to the mouth of the Paria River at Lees Ferry, Arizona. Its labyrinth of slickrock canyons were created by wind, freeze-thaw erosion, and thundering spring runoff and summer flash floods roaring down from the heights of the Henry Mountains, Rainbow Plateau, Navajo Mountain, Waterpocket Fold, Kaiparowits Plateau, and the perennial flows of the Escalante and San Juan Rivers. Among Glen Canyon's 100 serpentine canyons of Navajo Sandstone, many stand out for their incredible beauty, Native American migrations, Spanish and Mormon explorations, and historic Colorado River journeys. Paleo-Indian hunters and gatherers roamed here dating back to 11,500 BC, and Fremont and Ancestral Puebloans, and later the Hopi, Navajo, and Paiute, all made homes on the high mesas and in deep desert canyons. A once-secret example of the Ancestral Puebloans' ability to adapt to the raw environment far from larger pueblos like Mesa Verde and Chaco is Defiance House, where ancient cliff dwellers lived, prayed, and survived off the fruits of the land and river.

Scenic and Historic Mileposts

- **Defiance House, AD 1250.** Hidden from view for centuries in an alcove 300 feet above the Middle Fork of Forgotten Canyon, Defiance House was not officially discovered until 1959 when river runners Harry Aleson and Dick Sprang first visited and recorded the abandoned pueblo. "Defiance House" was later named by anthropology professor and archaeologist Jesse D. Jennings for the distinctive white pictographs of three warriors wielding shields and sticks on the painted wall above the dwellings. The small, defensive three-room pueblo was inhabited from AD 1250 to 1285 and is adjoined by an underground ceremonial kiva and food storage granaries.

BOATING ACCESS:
From Halls Crossing or Bullfrog Marinas: Navigate by boat or sea kayak from the main channel of Lake Powell, turn east between Buoys 107 and 106 (miles up-lake from Glen Canyon Dam) into the mouth of Forgotten Canyon, and pilot or paddle 3 miles up the Middle Fork to Defiance House.

- **Domínguez-Escalante Expedition, 1776, El Vado de Los Padres.** Unimaginable for many today, in 1776 Mexican and Spanish missionaries Francisco Atanasio Domínguez and Silvestre Vélez de Escalante explored a 1,700-mile route across the dangerous and uncharted terrain between Santa Fe, New Mexico, and Monterey, California. The approach of winter, famine, and thirst forced Domínguez and Escalante to try to return to Santa Fe. But the expedition became stranded below the walls of Paria Canyon near present-day Lees Ferry until a Paiute guide showed the padres the route through the treacherous cliffs. Searching for a way home, the indefatigable Franciscan explorers worked their way through the maze of canyons and mesas north of Glen Canyon, where they became stranded once again. Four days later a Ute guide showed them an old Indian route called the Ute Ford down Padre Creek, where the padres used axes to hack steps into the sandstone for their horses. After fording the Colorado River on November 7, Escalante named it "El Vado," later called *El Vado de Los Padres*, "The Crossing of the

Fathers." The party finally returned to Santa Fe 159 days after embarking on their historic quest. Now buried under Lake Powell, The Crossing of the Fathers is commemorated with a copper plaque that was bolted into a sandstone wall near the head of Padre Creek by members of the 1938 Julius F. Stone Glen Canyon river expedition.

BOATING ACCESS:

From Wahweap Marina: By boat or sea kayak, follow the main channel of Lake Powell, turn north at Buoy 15, and pilot or paddle to the head of Padre Creek.

■ **Navajo Medicine Man Blind Salt Clansman, Rainbow Bridge, 1863.** In a daring escape from Colonel Christopher Carson's troops, medicine man and Navajo chief *Hashkéniinii,* "Blind Salt Clansman," led 17 family members into the safety of the secret canyons encircling Navajo Mountain near Rainbow Bridge. In 1884, Hashkéniinii led prospectors J. Patterson Williams and his son W. F. Williams on a rugged overland journey to the largest natural bridge in the world.

HIKING AND BOATING ACCESS:

Hiking access from Rainbow Lodge site, Utah: See Rainbow Bridge National Monument entry on pages 59-63.

Boating access from Dangling Rope Marina: Navigating by boat or sea kayak from the main channel of Lake Powell, turn south at Buoy 49 into the mouth of Forbidding Canyon and pilot or paddle to Rainbow Bridge Canyon.

■ **Lees Ferry, 1871.** Located at the mouth of the Paria River at its confluence with the Colorado River, Lees Ferry and Lonely Dell ranch were homesteaded and developed in 1871 by Mormon pioneer and cattleman John Doyle Lee and his wife, Emma. Lee provided the only reliable ford across the Colorado River for hundreds of miles in both directions. It's nestled in a verdant *rincon,* or corner, of the Vermilion Cliffs and Paria Canyon where the Domínguez–Escalante Expedition was temporarily stranded in 1776. Located at river Mile 0, all expeditions going upstream or down use Lees Ferry as the "put-in" for their river journeys. Lees Ferry is listed on the National Register of Historic Places, and no visit to canyon country is complete without walking to this scenic outpost. Beneath the towering walls of Paria Canyon, you can view pioneer Warren Marshall Johnson's hand-hewn log cabin; an underground cellar or "dugout" for storing milk, cheese, butter, potatoes, and cabbages; the pioneer cemetery where Johnson laid to rest four of his children in 1871 after dying in his arms from diphtheria; the Weaver Ranch House built by Poli Hungavi, a Hopi stonemason, in 1935-1936; and a still thriving orchard of peaches, plums, and apricots.

HIKING ACCESS:

From the Navajo Bridge Interpretive Center: Drive east on U.S. Highway 89A and turn immediately right on the scenic Lees Ferry Road. Two miles from the highway junction, stop at the pullout on the left to see Balanced Rocks beneath the towering walls of Vermilion Cliffs National Monument. Drive 2 miles farther to reach the Lonely Dell/Paria Canyon Trailhead. Savor the self-guiding 1-mile round-trip hike that will take you back in time.

- **Hole in the Rock Expedition, 1879-1880.** Pioneering the harsh and rugged 180-mile-long cross-mesa-and-canyon Hole in the Rock Trail from Escalante to settle Bluff, Utah, the Mormon expedition led by Elias S. Smith included 250

Lees Ferry. PHOTO BY JOHN ANNERINO

HIKING AND BOATING ACCESS:

Hiking access from Escalante, Utah: Driving the route of pioneers in a high-clearance or 4WD vehicle, follow the 53.5-mile washboard Hole in the Rock Road past Forty Mile Spring and Dance Hall Rock to a remote trailhead on the edge of Gray Mesa. Overlooking Lake Powell, the 0.6-mile "trail" drops 2,000 vertical feet through a natural fissure called Uncle Ben's Dugway.

Boating access from Dangling Rope Marina: Navigating by boat or sea kayak from the main channel of Lake Powell, turn north at Buoy 66 and pilot or paddle to the foot of Gray Mesa.

men, women, and children who forged an astonishing route off the precipitous rim of Gray Mesa during the winter of 1879–1880. Using picks, shovels, and 1,000 pounds of dynamite, they chiseled a 0.5-mile-long, 25- to 45-degree "jump down" through a natural fault cleaved in the Navajo Sandstone. From the canyon rim, they lowered 83 heavy wooden wagons and drove 1,000 head of bawling and bleating livestock down to the stony banks of the Colorado River. In 1958, historian David E. Miller wrote in the *Utah Historical Quarterly* that it was "the most spectacular pioneer road-building project in the West." Hike this declivitous slickrock route with a heavy pack today and you'll appreciate the faith, pluck, and ingenuity of the hardy pioneers of yesteryear.

- **Navajo Bridge, 1929.** Viewed from the banks of the Colorado River in 1907, the Western novelist Zane Grey described the Navajo Bridge setting in his book, *The Last of the Plainsmen:* "I saw the constricted rapids, where

HIKING AND VISITOR ACCESS:

Due to a massive landslide, U.S. Highway 89 between Page and Bitter Springs, Arizona, is closed to through traffic.

From the north: From the junction of U.S. Highway 89 and North Lake Powell Boulevard, drive south 2.4 miles on U.S. 89 and turn left onto Arizona Highway 98. Drive 2.6 miles east on AZ 98 and turn right onto U.S. 89T. Drive 44 miles south on U.S. 89T and turn right onto U.S. 89. Drive 26 miles north on U.S. 89 and turn left onto U.S. 89A. Continue north 14.2 miles to the Colorado River and Navajo Bridge Interpretive Center on the right.

From the south: From the junction of U.S. Highways 160 and 89 just west of Tuba City, drive 42.6 miles north on U.S. 89. Go left at the junction with U.S. 89A and continue 14.2 miles north on U.S. 89A to the Colorado River and Navajo Bridge Interpretive Center on the right.

the Colorado took its plunge into the box-like head of the Grand Canyon of Arizona; and the deep, reverberating boom of the river, at flood height, was a fearful thing to hear. I could not repress a shudder at the thought of crossing above that rapid." Navajo horsemen called the crossing near Lees Ferry *Tó Ha'naant'eeliin*, "Where They Crossed Against the Current," and the Navajo high scalers and iron workers who riveted and welded together the 467-foot-high and 834-foot-long bridge in 1929 called it *Na'ní'á Hatsoh*, "Big Bridge." The original bridge is now a national historic monument. Replaced by the new Navajo Bridge in 1995, the historic bridge offers a spectacular pedestrian walkway high above the Colorado River flowing through Marble Canyon beneath the jagged cinnamon-red skyline of Echo Peaks.

■ **Major John Wesley Powell, 1869 and 1950s-1960s.** John Wesley Powell, a Union Army major who had his right arm shot off with a mini ball during the Civil War Battle of Shiloh, led seven other daring men on a 930-mile expedition down the largely unexplored Green and Colorado Rivers from Green River, Wyoming, to the Virgin River, Nevada. Like the Domínguez-Escalante Expedition 93 years earlier, the Powell expedition was destined to be an extraordinary journey in the annals of American history. In Powell's river journal, later published in *Exploration of the Colorado River of the West*, his July 31, 1869, entry names and describes Glen Canyon's beauty: "The walls are steadily increasing in altitude, the curves are gentle, and often the river sweeps by an arc of vertical wall, smooth and unbroken, and then by a curve that is variegated by royal arches, mossy alcoves, deep, beautiful glens, and painted grottoes."

Many explorers, prospectors, and river runners since have been captivated by Glen Canyon's comely charm and sublimity, including Katie Lee, who was one of the last to row through the "beautiful glens" in the 1950s and 1960s that were soon buried by the dam and lamented by legions of others who fell in love with the canyon's natural wonders. In her book, *All My Rivers Are Gone: A Journey of Discovery Through Glen Canyon*, Lee describes the caress of sandstone on her fingers: "A sensuous frequency ripples through me as my hand touches those silken curves, hollows, and convolutions on a body of stone . . . ." Photographer Tad Nichols was also held rapt by Glen Canyon, sometimes joining Katie Lee on river journeys and explorations that resulted in Nichols' evocative collection of black-and-white images published decades later in *Glen Canyon: Images of a Lost World, Photographs and Recollections.* You can rediscover Glen Canyon through the pages of Lee's and Nichols' books, and the colorful gallery of

HIKING AND BOATING ACCESS:

Hiking access from Page, Arizona: Drive 3 miles south on U.S. Highway 89 past Milepost 545 to the unmarked turnoff on the right to Horseshoe Bend. From the parking area, hike along an abandoned road 0.75 mile west to the exposed vista.

Boating access from Lees Ferry: Paddle or row 15.6 miles upstream or hire a ride, ferry, or tow. Visit Colorado River Discovery, ,raftthecanyon.com/.

images in Elliot Porter's reissued 1963 book, *The Place No One Knew: Glen Canyon on the Colorado.*

And you can see what the author described as "the last surviving relic of this mysterious canyon" at Horseshoe Bend. From the vista, you'll be greeted with a panoramic view of Echo Peaks on the western horizon and the tranquil waters of the Colorado River 1,200 feet below your feet. Flowing through Nine Mile Bar, the storied river loops around the terracotta walls of Navajo Sandstone in a 270-degree horseshoe turn and flows through Glen Canyon to Lees Ferry. Better yet, you can paddle or row this quiet stretch. Start with a motorized upstream run from Lees Ferry to carry

Horseshoe Bend. PHOTO BY JOHN ANNERINO

your party, kayaks, rafts, dories, and canoes to the launch site. Then take your time to gaze in wonder, picnic, camp, and explore Ancestral Puebloan rock art and dwellings.

■ **Glen Canyon Dam, 1964.** This 710-foot-tall concrete arch dam was built by 2,500 workers over eight years at the cost of $107,955,552. Glen Canyon Dam was completed in 1964, but Lake Powell did not fill to "full pool" capacity at 3,700-feet until 1980. Three years later, runoff from heavy snowpack in the Colorado River upper basin states of Utah, New Mexico, Colorado, and Wyoming threatened to breach the controversial engineering feat that is still loved and hated today. For a riveting history, read the late author Marc Reisner's nonfiction book, *Cadillac Desert: The American West and Its Disappearing Water.*

HIKING AND BOATING ACCESS:

Hiking access: For guided tours of Glen Canyon Dam, visit the Glen Canyon Natural History Association at www.glencanyonnha.org/glen_canyon_dam/glencanyondam_tour.php.

Boating access: For access information to Bullfrog, Halls Crossing, Hite, Dangling Rope, and Wahweap Marinas, and guided tours of Glen Canyon and Lake Powell, visit the Glen Canyon Natural History Association at www.nps.gov/glca/parkmgmt/concessionaires.htm.

Glen Canyon Tributary

■ **Lower Antelope Canyon, 2013.** Of Glen Canyon's 100 named tributary canyons, none is more beautiful than the symphony of stone and light the Navajo call *Hasdestwazi*, "Spiral Rock Arches." Only the hands of gods and the natural forces of wind, rain, sand, and violent flash floods could sculpt stone with such form and elegance. Illuminated with the spectral refractions of sun-, moon-, and starlight, here is a natural underground kiva where you can walk, dance, and chant to the rhythms of the stones. Nor are any of Glen Canyon's sublime earth cracks as dangerous. On August 1, 1997, ignoring impending storm warnings and flash flood dangers, 12 canyoneers were swept to their deaths in an unforgiving and inescapable wall of water that roared through the crack all the way to Glen Canyon. After that tragedy, Navajo rancher and photographer Ken Young took it upon himself to rig metal safety ladders for the short canyon descent and emergency escape options.

HIKING AND VISITOR ACCESS:

From Page, Arizona: From the intersection of U.S. Highway 89T and Arizona Highway 98 south of Page, drive 2.2 miles east on AZ 98. Turn left onto Antelope Point Road/BIA 222 and drive 0.5 mile north. Turn left again, drive 0.3 mile south, and turn right into the Lower Antelope Canyon turnoff and parking area.

Hiking permits and tours: Visit Lower Antelope Canyon Tours, www.lowerantelope.com/.

Lower Antelope Canyon. PHOTO BY JOHN ANNERINO

Betatakin cliff dwelling. PHOTO BY JOHN ANNERINO

NAVAJO NATIONAL MONUMENT

Landscape, People, and Culture

Surrounded by the stunning landscapes of Monument Valley, Navajo Mountain, and Black Mesa, the 7,400-foot-high piñon- and juniper-covered Shonto Plateau is cut by deeply incised canyons that drain into the Goosenecks of the San Juan River near Utah's Valley of the Gods. Principal among these ruggedly beautiful canyons is Tsegi Canyon and its tributaries: Dowozhiebito, Keet Seel, and Long Canyons. These canyons hold huge alcoves sculpted in sheer walls of Navajo Sandstone by wind erosion, rockfall, ceiling collapses, and flash floods 180 million years ago.

Ancient hunters known as Archaic peoples found shelter in these cave-like oases in the high, arid Painted Desert. They depended on sweet water from semi-perennial streams and crystal water seeps that trickled through the cross-bedded Navajo Sandstone and formed a spring line at its contact with the impermeable Kayenta Formation. Ancestral Puebloans built kivas, storage granaries, and multi-storied cliff dwellings in these protective, spring-fed alcoves that were later used by ancestral Hopi, San Juan Paiute, Zuni, and Navajo.

Only five precious springs supported cliff dwellers at Betatakin, Keet Seel, and Inscription House, where they hunted, gathered, and tilled terraced plots of irrigated corn, beans, and squash from AD 1250 to 1300. When the Navajo, or Diné, migrated into the region, they called these magnificent places *Bitát'ahkin*, "House on a Rock Ledge," *Kits'iil*, "Shattered House," and *Ts'ah Biis Kin*, "House in the Sage Brush" (today known as Inscription House). Other dwellings included Bat Woman, Turkey Cave, and Swallows Nest.

Among these "cliff cities," as early travel writer George Wharton James described them, the 160-room Keet Seel is the largest cliff dwelling in the United States. It was "discovered" by Richard Wetherill and Charles Mason in 1895, while looking for an independent-minded mule named Neephi.

President William Howard Taft established Navajo National Monument under the Antiquities Act on March 20, 1909, to preserve the area's cultural legacy. The monument now includes three small areas within Navajo lands: Betatakin in Betatakin Canyon, Keet Seel in Keet Seel Canyon, and Inscription House in Nitsin Canyon 16 miles to the west.

When George Wharton James first visited Betatakin on horseback with a Navajo guide in 1917, he wrote in *Arizona, The Wonderland*, "It was not the mass of ruins that gripped me . . . It was the vastness, the stupendousness, the tremendously impressive natural arch that arose above Betatakin."

Come walk with reverence in the footsteps of ancient cliff dwellers and contemplate their life ways, culture, and the extraordinary architecture of their multi-storied canyon dwellings we have emulated in the steel canyons of America's modern cities.

Hiking

Short, self-guided walks follow Sandal, Aspen, and Canyon View Trails, all leaving from behind the visitor center. To reach Betatakin and Keet Seel cliff

DRIVING AND HIKING ACCESS:

From the north: From the junction of U.S. Highways 160 and 163 in Kayenta, Arizona, drive 19.2 miles west on U.S. 160 and turn right onto Arizona Highway 564. Drive 9.4 miles north to the visitor center.

From the south: From the junction of U.S. Highways 160 and 89, drive 62.7 miles northwest on U.S. 160 and turn left onto Arizona Highway 564. Drive 9.4 miles north to the visitor center.

dwellings, you must register for ranger-guided tours (free), available only from May to September. Also, a hiking permit (free) is required for the 17-mile round-trip trek to Keet Seel. Advance reservations are advised, especially during summer and on weekends. Rockfall, flash floods, and quicksand are potential hazards.

- **Sandal Trail.** The self-guiding, 1.3-mile round-trip hike on a paved trail from the visitor center offers spectacular rim-top views of Betatakin from the precipitous overlook nearly 1,000 feet above. After the long drive to reach the monument and setting up camp, stretch your legs on this enjoyable walk atop the slickrock. It's a good warm-up before setting out on the Betatakin or Keet Seel hike the next day. Sunsets along the rim are memorable.

- **Tsegi Point Trail to Betatakin Trail.** The Tsegi Point Trailhead is 0.75 mile north of the visitor center. Starting at an elevation of 7,272 feet, this ranger-guided 5-mile round-trip hike follows an old road along Tsegi Point to a rocky trail that switchbacks 700 feet down to the trail junction of Keet Seel and Betatakin Canyons. Turn right to follow the trail up Betatakin Canyon through groves of piñon, juniper, aspen, and Gambel oak below cliffs of Navajo Sandstone to the short, steep trail up to stairsteps chiseled in stone that were once used to reach the cliff dwellings. The enormous alcove, as measured by early surveyors, is 452 feet high and 370 feet wide and echoes the sounds of raptors and visitors alike. Betatakin's breathtaking multi-tiered cliff dwellings include 135 rooms, storage granaries, kivas, and

Betatakin close-up. PHOTO BY JOHN ANNERINO

Hopi Fire Clan pictograph. PHOTO BY JOHN ANNERINO

seed grinding stones used by a clan of 75 to 100 people from AD 1250 to 1300. Tall ladders made from wooden timbers are still propped against ancient walls as if they were used yesterday. On an alcove wall is the sacred ancestral Hopi symbol of *Kókopnyam*, "Fire Clan," who dwelled in Betatakin and Tsegi Canyons. Oswald White Bear Fredericks, a Hopi artist and collector of oral histories that became the basis for Frank Waters' *Book of the Hopi*, said that, together, the three cliff dwellings now within Navajo National Monument were called *Kawéstima*, "Village in the North," and were said to be the home of *Katsina*, "Spirit Beings." In 1909, returning from their explorations of Inscription House and Keet Seel, Oljato Trading Post owners John Wetherill, his wife Louisa, and archaeologist Byron L. Cummings stopped at the Tsegi Canyon hogan of Nedi Cloey and hired his Navajo son-in-law to guide them 2 miles to the hidden cliff dwelling they visited and named *"Bitát'ahkin"* on August 9, 1909. Rockfall and flash floods are potential hazards. Advance reservations are advised.

- **Tsegi Point Trail to Keet Seel Trail.** A hiking permit is required, available at the visitor center. The Tsegi Point Trailhead is 0.75 mile north of the visitor center. The 17-mile round-trip trek follows the same abandoned road along Tsegi Point to the rocky trail that switchbacks 700 vertical feet down to the trail junction of Keet Seel and Betatakin Canyons. Turn left and use your orienteering skills to hike cross-country through Keet Seel Canyon. You must ford the braided stream many times and your shoes

Keet Seel. PHOTO BY NPS

Corn grinding stones. PHOTO BY JOHN ANNERINO

will get wet. White mileposts mark the route for the next 3 miles. The last 5.5 miles climbs 400 vertical feet to the Keet Seel Ranger Station and Campground. Go to the ranger station to request a tour of the dwelling. Bring a pair of soft-soled camp shoes to help minimize damage to the fragile cliff dwelling. The Hopi word *Kawéstima* is often ascribed to Keet Seel, and in the *Hopi Dictionary* it's defined as the "Kachina home representing the northwest cardinal direction." Inhabited by an estimated 150 people from AD 950 to 1250, Ancestral Puebloans dwelled in 160 rooms, chanted and danced in six ceremonial kivas, and sealed off their food storage granaries of corn when they abandoned the area. The primitive campground sleeps 20. Rockfall and flash floods are potential hazards. Advance reservations are advised.

■ **Inscription House.** Guided to Inscription House by a local Navajo man named Pinieten or Hosteen Jones, John Wetherill, archaeologist Byron L. Cummings, and their party visited this cliff dwelling in 1909. The 74-room Inscription House is known to the Hopi as *Tsu'ovi,* "Place of the Rattlesnakes." Professor Cummings named it "Inscription House" after three of the party's children unearthed the mysterious inscription *Anno Domini 1661.* The Latin phrase translates to "in the year of our Lord," and the carving was initially thought to be the handiwork of Spanish explorers, but it has also been attributed to 19th-century Mormon pioneers. Inscription House is closed to the public due to erosion, rockfall, ceiling collapses, and privacy concerns with nearby private homes. It is still used by Native Americans for spiritual purposes and ceremonies.

Sunset View Campground and Loop Road. Tucked in a forest of piñon and juniper about 200 yards southwest of the visitor center, this campground offers 30 campsites, picnic tables, restrooms, water, and convenient access to the Sandal Trail.

Canyon View Campground. This campground is 0.1 mile north of the visitor center. It offers composting toilets and charcoal grills, but no water. Of the 16 sites, 3 can accommodate groups with space for up to 15 tents.

Hiking Permits. For hiking permits, visit the Navajo National Monument website at www.nps.gov/nava/planyourvisit/permits.htm.

White House cliff dwelling. PHOTO BY JOHN ANNERINO

CANYON DE CHELLY NATIONAL MONUMENT

Landscape, People, and Culture

Located in the heart of the Four Corners region of *Dinétah*, or Navajoland, Canyon de Chelly (de-SHAY) figures prominently in the Diné's spiritual landscape within the cardinal directions of its four sacred mountains, which are *Dibé nitsaa*, "Big Mountain Sheep," or Hesperus Peak in Colorado's La Plata Range in the north; *Sisnaajiní*, "Horizontal Black Belt," or Blanca Peak in Colorado's Sangre de Cristo Mountains in the east; *Dootizhii dziil*, "Turquoise Mountain," or Mount Taylor in New Mexico's San Mateo Mountains in the south; and *Dook'o'oslííd*, "Never Thaws on Top," or San Francisco Peaks in Arizona's San Francisco Mountains in the west. Navajo medicine men known as *ha'athali*, or "singers," make pilgrimages to these mythic mountains where gods still dwell. There, they collect sacred earth, plants, stones of obsidian, abalone, and turquoise, as well as white shells, carrying them in *dzileezh bijish*, or "medicine pouches," used in traditional age-old blessings, chants, and ceremonies. Their trails lead in the four directions and include many sacred springs, rivers, buttes, canyons, and mountains that medicine men identified for Aboriginal Title with the Indian Claims Commission Act of 1946. Known among the Diné as *Tséyi'*, "In Between the Rocks," Canyon de Chelly has been continuously inhabited for nearly 5,000 years—longer than any other place on the Colorado Plateau. Today, about 40 Navajo families still live within the canyons here, farming and raising livestock.

The monument covers 83,840 acres of the 7,622-foot-high Defiance Plateau, where ponderosa pine forests and grassland savannahs are drained to the west by the precipitous De Chelly Sandstone chasms of Canyon de Chelly, Canyon del Muerto, and their tributaries: Bat, Monument, and Black Rock Canyons. Together they form a spectacular landscape of deep interwoven canyons lush with perennial water and groves of cottonwood trees. Here Archaic peoples hunted abundant wildlife and gathered plentiful natural foods and medicinal plants between 2,500 and 500 BC. Ancestral Puebloans later built 138 magnificent cliff dwellings in protective niches and alcoves in the sheer walls of De Chelly Sandstone. Striking patinas of desert varnish cascade over the canyon walls from rims high above; the same walls are alive with rock art. The pastoral agriculturalists inhabited the area between AD 1060 and 1275 and grew corn, beans, and squash until ancestral Hopi and later the Navajo migrated into area.

As idyllic as this riparian oasis in the Painted Desert was, it attracted a scourge of Spanish, Mexican, and American raids that destroyed orchards, fields, and livestock and maimed and killed many Navajos during the 1700s and 1800s. On the bright side, the *bahana*, "white man," was irresistibly drawn to the spectacular and spiritual realm of Canyon de Chelly, and this led to the eventual protection of the area and people.

Working for the U.S. Army Corps of Engineers (then in the War Department) in 1873, pioneer photographer Timothy H. O'Sullivan took the first images of the picturesque sandstone walls, which drew legions of other photographers. Chief among them was Edward S. Curtis, hailed by the *New York Times* as an "American hero and the world's most celebrated photographer of Native Americans." Curtis' iconic black-and-white photo, *Canyon de Chelly - Navaho*,

DRIVING AND HIKING ACCESS:

From U.S. Highway 191 in Chinle, Arizona: Drive 3 miles east on Indian Route 7 to the visitor center. Just east of the visitor center, the road forks: to the right is South Rim Drive and to the left is North Rim Drive.

1904, is the single most sought after image in the Curtis Collection of 50,000 negatives. Dwarfed by the looming walls of Canyon de Chelly, Curtis' image of seven Navajo riding horseback through the shallow waters of Chinle Wash has become an indelible symbol of the West.

In 1906, celebrated author and Indian rights activist Charles F. Lummis explored Canyon de Chelly, guided by Indian trader, Navajo friend, and owner of the Ganado trading post John Lorenzo Hubbell. In the 1907 *Out West* magazine feature, "The Swallow's-Nest People," Lummis described the environs of White House cliff dwelling he called *Casa Blanca*, which he'd viewed from the canyon floor: "Few whites ever see this marvelous scenery with its wonderful remains of the Swallow's Nest People of Long Ago. Sometimes they are only an arrow-flight above the water; sometimes so high in the beetling rocks that only an eagle eye can make them out, and that only one with the foot of the mountain sheep can still climb to them."

The incomparable canyon scenery also drew the attention of Hollywood director J. Lee Thompson. Based on Will Henry's bestselling novel, *MacKenna's Gold*, Thompson filmed the star-studded 1969 Western in Canyon de Chelly,

White House cliff dwelling.   PHOTO BY JOHN ANNERINO

with Gregory Peck playing the American gold seeker MacKenna, Omar Sharif as the mustached Mexican outlaw Colorado, and Julie Newmar as the beautiful Apache maiden Hesh-Ke. In the cinematic tale of lost gold guarded by "Apache" gods, the 800-foot-tall, twin-columned Spider Rock beneath Arachnid Mesa became "Shaking Rock." Home of *Na'acdjeii 'esdzaa,* or "Spider Woman," central to the Shooting Chant Ceremony, Spider Rock cast a long, mysterious shadow across the valley that the gold seekers traced on horseback into a hidden passage that led to Canyon de Chelly, or *Cañon del Oro,* "Canyon of Gold." The climactic fight scene between MacKenna and Colorado takes place at an ancient cliff-top ruin high above Cañon del Oro's thick veins of pure gold.

Established on April 1, 1931, by President Herbert Hoover to protect Native America's cultural legacy, Canyon de Chelly National Monument is unique in the National Park System because it is located on Navajo Trust Land.

White House cliff dwelling. PHOTO BY JOHN ANNERINO

Hiking

White House Trail. The trailhead is at the White House Overlook 6 miles east of the visitor center on the South Rim Drive. This is the only trail in the monument open to hiking without a Navajo guide.

From the trailhead, the 1.25-mile sheepherder's trail snakes across the slickrock through two tunnels and past declivitous sections blasted out by Civilian Conservation Corps-Indian Service workers in 1936. Savor the panoramic vistas from the airy path that descends 600 vertical feet to the floor of Chinle Wash. Called the *'Asdzání Hanitiin,* "Woman's Trail Up," the White House Trail is one of 11 ancestral trails located and identified by geologist and cultural geographer Dr. Stephen C. Jett in his American Indian Studies publication, *Navajo Placenames and Trails of the Canyon de Chelly System, Arizona.* When you reach the canyon floor, you'll have a fenced-off but close-up canyon view of one of the most spectacular cliff dwellings on the Colorado Plateau. Called *Kin níí' na' igaih,* "White House In Between," by the Navajo, White House cliff dwelling is on the National Register of Historic Places. If you study the wall between the 60-room, 6-kiva ruins on the canyon floor and the 20-room White House cliff dwelling 30 feet above, you'll see white pictographs. One is an anthropomorphic figure that may be a *katsina,* "Spirit Being," or kachina. It may have been painted by Hopi ancestors called the *Hisat.sinom,* "People Who Lived Long Ago," who lived here until AD 1278. The dwelling place of mythic deities called *Yéi Becheii,* White House was also sacred to Navajo medicine men who performed the Night Chant healing ceremony here until the 1940s. During the height of summer tourist season, expect bustling 4WD traffic from canyon tourist shuttles and Native American artists and vendors offering handmade, intricately designed clay pots, hand-carved and painted cottonwood kachina figures, and handmade silver and turquoise jewelry.

Scenic Drives

South Rim Drive (Indian Route 7). From the visitor center at an elevation of 5,510 feet, the paved 32-mile round-trip scenic drive leads to a turnaround at Spider Rock Overlook (elevation 6,871 feet). At about 12 miles from the visitor center, follow the pavement left; the entire route is also popular with bicyclists. Allow 2 to 3 hours to see all seven viewpoints overlooking Canyon de Chelly.

- **Stop 1:** Tunnel Overlook pullout on left.
- **Stop 2:** Tsegi Canyon Overlook pullout on left. ADA accessible.

- **Stop 3: Junction Overlook turnoff on left.** Views of the verdant confluence of Canyon de Chelly and Canyon del Muerto, and the 10-room Junction Ruin. ADA accessible.

- **Stop 4: White House Overlook and Trailhead turnoff on left.** Drive 0.7 mile to the parking lot. A 2.5-mile round-trip trail to White House cliff dwelling (see White House Trail entry). Overlook is ADA accessible.

- **Stop 5: Sliding House Overlook turnoff on left.** Drive 1.6 miles to the parking lot. Views of Sliding House Ruin, which has 30 to 50 rooms.

- **Stop 6: Face Rock Overlook pullout on left.** Views of Face Rock.

- **Stop 7: Spider Rock Overlook pullout on left (elevation 6,871 feet).** Views of Spider Rock, confluence of Bat Canyon and Canyon de Chelly, and Defiance Plateau. ADA accessible.

North Rim Drive (Diné Tah "Among the People" Scenic Road, Indian Route 64). From the visitor center, the paved 36-mile round-trip scenic drive leads to the Massacre Cave Overlook. The route is also popular with bicyclists. Allow 2 to 3 hours to see all three viewpoints overlooking Canyon del Muerto.

- **Stop 1: Antelope House Overlook turnoff on right.** Drive 1.9 miles to the parking lot. Views of Antelope House Ruin.

- **Stop 2: Mummy Cave Overlook turnoff on right.** Drive 0.75 mile to where the road forks and turn right. Continue 1.4 miles to the overlook. Views of Mummy Ruin.

- **Stop 3: Massacre Cave Overlook turnoff on right.** From the same turnoff on Indian Route 64, at the road fork, turn left and drive 1.3 miles to the overlook. Views of Massacre Cave, Yucca Ruin, and Mummy Ruin. ADA accessible.

Spaniards coming to the Canyon. PHOTO BY JOHN ANNERINO

Guided 4WD Tours of Canyon de Chelly and Canyon del Muerto

Navajo guided tours start at the visitor center and last 3 to 7 hours. Check with your guides beforehand to see what stops they'll be making.

Canyon de Chelly. Popular sites

that can be seen or visited are First Ruin, Junction Ruin, White House Ruins, Sliding House Ruin, and Spider Rock.

Canyon del Muerto. Popular sites that can be seen or visited are Junction Ruin, Ledge Ruin, Antelope House Ruin and pictographs, Navajo Fortress, Standing Cow Ruin, and Mummy Cave Ruin.

Canyon Tours
Visit Canyon de Chelly Tours at canyondechellytours.com/.
Visit the National Park Service list of tour companies at www.nps.gov/cach/planyourvisit/loader.cfm?csModule=security/getfile&pageID=632254.

Cottonwood Campground. Located 0.25 mile southwest of the visitor center, this primitive campground in a grove of cottonwoods offers 93 campsites with parking, picnic tables, grills, and three restrooms.

Mummy house. PHOTO BY JOHN ANNERINO

Bluffs above Wahweap Creek. PHOTO BY JOHN ANNERINO

GRAND STAIRCASE- ESCALANTE NATIONAL MONUMENT

Landscape, People, and Culture

Named for the stratigraphy of its colorful geography and the explorations of missionaries Silvestre Vélez de Escalante and Francisco Atanasio Domínguez in 1776, Grand Staircase is a stark, colorful, and dramatic landscape within the "Grand Circle" of the padres' epic 1,700-mile route across the Four Corners' vast *despoblado*, or "uninhabited land." The stunning physiography of Grand Staircase's kaleidoscopic terrain includes three distinct areas characterized by high deserts, deep canyons, magnificent cliffs, and forested peaks and plateaus. The western Grand Staircase section was first described by geologist Clarence E. Dutton in his 1882 magnum opus, *Tertiary History Grand Canyon District.* Surveying the unmapped region under the direction of Major John Wesley Powell, Dutton wrote that the geology from the Kaibab uplift climbed "like a great stairway" through the Vermilion, Chocolate, White,

Rainbow over Grand Staircase. PHOTO BY JOHN ANNERINO

Gray, and Pink Cliffs 6,000 feet up to the hoodoo rim of Bryce Canyon's 9,115-foot Paunsaugunt Plateau. The middle Kaiparowits Plateau section, named for the Southern Paiute, who viewed it as *Kaivavic*, or "Mountain Lying Down," is a triangular 1,650-square-mile landmass wedged between the escarpments of the Cockscomb, Straight Cliffs, and Fiftymile Mountain. Gushing down from its headwaters atop the 11,328-foot Aquarius Plateau, the 87-mile eastern Escalante River Canyons section drains into the Colorado River in Glen Canyon, creating a 1,000-square-mile labyrinth of water-scoured slickrock canyons like no place on Earth.

Dating back 6,000 years, Grand Staircase's cultural legacy includes Archaic peoples, contemporaneously Fremont and Ancestral Puebloans, and later the Numic-speaking Escalante band of Southern Paiute called the *Kwaguiuavi*, or "Seed Valley People." In the piñon-juniper forests crowning the 7,956-foot Kaiparowits Plateau, they depended on natural springs and seasonal shelters in caves and wikiups where they slept in rabbit skin robes and bearskin blankets. They gathered elderberries and serviceberries that they ground on metates, and hunted desert bighorn sheep, mule deer, and pronghorn with sinew-backed juniper bows and stone-tipped willow arrows. The meat was spit roasted or sun-jerked, and the hides were scraped and tanned into buckskin clothing and moccasins. The Southern Paiute's ancestral names throughout this remote and marvelous quarter of the Four Corners brings cultural richness to Grand Staircase's storied places and landmarks. Comprising 1.9 million acres, Grand Staircase-Escalante National Monument was established under the 1906 Antiquities Act by President William J. Clinton on September 18, 1996.

Scenic and Historic Mileposts

- **Devils Garden, 1872, The Goblins.** Formed 160 million years ago, the strange-looking, Jurassic-aged hoodoos, goblins, and arches are comprised of multicolored layers of the Gunsight Butte, Cannonville, and Escalante Members of Entrada Sandstone. One of the first parties to explore the area was the 1872 Powell Survey, which "discovered" the Escalante River, reported to be "the last major river discovered in the United States." Led by professor, explorer, and geologist Almon Harris Thompson, the horseback expedition stopped at Devils Garden while searching for the Dirty Devil River where Major John Wesley Powell's Colorado River expedition had cached a boat in 1869. Accompanying Thompson's overland expedition was photographer John K. "Jack" Hillers, who photographed the hoodoos Thompson called "Goblins." Following Thompson's lead, Hillers later named Metate Arch "Goblins Archway." Encountering four Mormon pioneers during their arduous journey, Hillers wrote that they were "talking about making a settlement here. [I] Advised them to call the place Escalante." Many years later one of Escalante's native sons, Edson B. Alvey, a naturalist, amateur archaeologist, and science teacher, explored the Escalante River area, sometimes to the delight of schoolchildren he brought along on field trips that included the fanciful location Alvey named "Devils Garden." By any

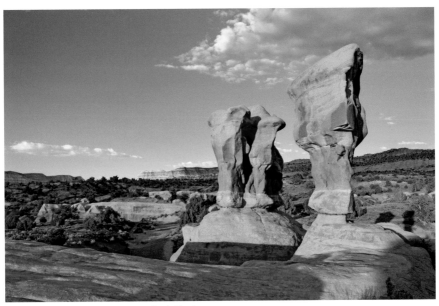

Devils Garden. PHOTO BY JOHN ANNERINO

DRIVING AND HIKING ACCESS:

From the Escalante Interagency Visitor Center in Escalante, Utah: Drive 6 miles east on Utah Scenic Byway 12 to the Hole-in-the-Rock Road junction. Set your odometer, turn right on the Hole-in-the-Rock Road and drive 10.2 miles on the washboard dirt road to the Devils Garden turnoff. Turn right and drive 0.3 mile to the parking area, access trail, restroom, and picnic sites.

name, a self-guiding 0.5-mile walk along the sandy trails winding through this whimsical garden of stone makes for a wonderful family outing.

- **Hole in the Rock Trail, 1935, Everett Ruess.** Many adventurers, canyoneers, river runners, and writers who've been drawn to canyon country first heard the siren call of Everett Ruess. The 20-year-old poet and painter roamed the back of beyond with a string of burros from California's high Sierra Nevada to Arizona and Utah's sprawling Monument Valley. During his journeys of quiet solitude through landscapes of breathless beauty, Ruess carved woodblocks for printing, painted the roseate deserts, canyons, and mesas with oils and watercolors, and wrote memorable letters to his family. One telling, postmarked dispatch read: *"Say that I starved; that I was lost and weary; That I was burned and blinded by the desert sun; Footsore, thirsty, sick with strange diseases; Lonely and wet and cold, but that I kept my dream!"* On November 12, 1934, Ruess rode out of Escalante leading a pack string of burros and followed the historic Hole-in-the-Rock Trail forged across the Escalante Desert by Mormon pioneers. Then *pfft!* he vanished.

The seasoned wilderness traveler and packer was last seen by a Navajo sheepherder on November 19, and four months later two of his half-starved burros were found in Davis Gulch, a tributary of the Colorado River within reach of the Hole-in-the-Rock Trail. From that point on, Davis Gulch marked the X on the map for searchers who looked for clues and physical evidence of Ruess' disappearance. They studied between the lines of his handwritten letters and read the series of news accounts published in the *Los Angeles Times*. In a front-page headline in the June 15, 1952, Sunday edition news feature, "Utah Canyons Veil Fate of L.A. Poet, Everett Ruess' Literary Artistic Promise Lost in His Beloved Wilderness 18 Years Ago," reporter Norris Leap wrote, "Mystery haunts the name of Everett Ruess." It

DRIVING AND HIKING ACCESS:

From the Escalante Interagency Visitor Center in Escalante, Utah: Drive 6 miles east on Utah Scenic Byway 12 to the Hole-in-the-Rock Road junction. Set your odometer, turn right on Hole-in-the-Rock Road and drive 50.5 miles on the high-clearance road to Fiftymile Creek. Cross the creek and park in an unmarked flat area on the south side of the road. The route to Davis Gulch is unmarked and requires cross-country route-finding skills. Ask for specific directions at the visitor center in Escalante.

still does to this day. Some speculated he was killed by an "Indian renegade," or he slipped and fell off a cliff, drowned while crossing the Colorado River to see a Navajo girlfriend, or disappeared into Old Mexico. More recent magazine coverage suggested that disinterred skeletal remains found by Navajos were those of Ruess, but DNA testing refuted the claim, and nothing stuck. Following up on a 1936 news account of a canyon country double murder, and clues discovered by river runner Ken Sleight 40 miles distant from Davis Gulch, mystery writer Chuck Greaves followed the possibilities on foot through Johnson Canyon, where he believes Ruess may have met his fate at the hands of an escaped fugitive.

The author of the environmental axiom, "Leave No Trace," Everett Ruess is alive and well in the legends and mysteries of the American West. Gumshoe the unsolved mystery yourself and retrace the poet's tracks from Escalante to the canyon rim above the X on the map in Davis Gulch.

■ **Kodachrome Basin State Park, 1947, National Geographic.** Ancestral lands of Southern Paiute, Kodachrome Basin State Park comprises 2,240 acres of a piñon juniper slickrock basin in the high desert east of Bryce Canyon. Unique among Kodachrome Basin's geology are 67 spires that formed over 180 million years when ancient geysers erupted through the multi-hued Gunsight Butte, Cannonville, and Escalante Members of Entrada Sandstone and created sedimentary "sand pipes" 6 to 170 feet tall. Homesteaded by

Monolith, Kodachrome Basin State Park. PHOTO BY JOHN ANNERINO

DRIVING AND HIKING ACCESS:

From the national monument visitor center in Cannonville, Utah: Drive 6 miles south on Main Street, which becomes Kodachrome Way and then Cottonwood Canyon Road. Turn left on Kodachrome Basin Road at the sign for Kodachrome Basin State Park and drive 0.9 mile to the visitor center on the right.

Mormon pioneers during the 1870s, the basin was first known as Thorley's Pasture after rancher Tom Thorley, who established a ranch in the remote area during the 1930s. Henrieville cowboys who drove cattle over the rocky divide to graze Indian ricegrass, needlegrass, and corral grass thick with prickly pear cactus called it "Thorny Pasture." The name changed in 1947 when *National Geographic* magazine launched a motorized expedition through the captivating Escalante Desert. Shooting Kodachrome film, photographer and writer Jack Breed called the colorful basin of spires and sand pipes "Kodachrome Flat." After Breed's 1949 feature, "First Motor Sortie into Escalante Land," was published in the magazine, the name stuck, with the nod of the Kodak Film Company. More than 11 miles of gentle to challenging hiking trails lead from the campground to the landmarks,

stone hallways, and "aha" viewpoints of Angels Palace, Shakespeare Arch, Big Bear Geysers, and other destinations. The Grand Parade and Panorama Trails are also open to horses and bicycles. The 0.5-mile hard-surface Nature Trail provides interpretive panels on the area's plants, animals, and geology, and is ADA accessible.

■ **Grosvenor Arch, 1947, National Geographic.** Ten miles down the road from Kodachrome Basin is the towering double-windowed Grosvenor Arch. Called the Butler Valley Arch by Henrieville and Cannonville locals and cowboys, it formed in Henrieville Sandstone and was renamed by the 1949 Escalante Land expedition after National Geographic Society founder Gilbert C. Grosvenor. The double arch soars 152 feet tall and spans 92 feet.

Grosvenor Arch. PHOTO BY JOHN ANNERINO

DRIVING AND HIKING ACCESS:

From the national monument visitor center in Cannonville, Utah:
Drive 6 miles south on Main Street, which becomes Kodachrome Way and then Cottonwood Canyon Road. At 6 miles, pass the turnoff to Kodachrome Basin State Park and the pavement's end, and continue east on Cottonwood Canyon Road. At 16.7 miles the road forks; stay left and drive another 1 mile to the Grosvenor Arch Day Use Area on the left. An ADA-accessible hard-surface path leads from the parking lot, restrooms, and picnic tables north 160 yards to the base of the arch.

Vermilion Cliffs National Monument

Ringed by Grand Staircase-Escalante National Monument, Glen Canyon National Recreation Area, Kaibab National Forest, and nearby Grand Canyon National Park, this 280,000-acre gem is rugged, remote, and relatively un-spoiled. Forty percent of the area is designated wilderness. Characterized by towering cliffs and deep canyons, the monument is home to desert bighorn sheep, mule deer, coyotes, foxes, bobcats, mountain lions, chuckwallas and other lizards, bald and golden eagles, peregrine falcons, and California condors.

■ **Paria Canyon, 1871, John D. Lee Cattle Drive.** Called *Paria Pa*, or "Elk Water," by the Kaibab Band of Southern Paiute, the 47-mile, 3,233-foot-deep Paria Canyon forms one of the Grand Canyon's four longest and deepest tributaries. Arguably one of the most beautiful and sinuous canyons in North America, Paria Canyon drains 1,570 square miles of the Kaiparowits

California condor. PHOTO BY JENNY EBERLEIN, NPS

Young hiker, Paria Canyon. PHOTO BY JOHN ANNERINO

Plateau and was a migration corridor for Ancestral Puebloans. Cattleman and pioneer John D. Lee drove 54 head of cattle down the Paria's ice-choked narrows during a freezing eight-day cattle drive that ranks as one of the most remarkable in the American West. Geologist Herbert E. Gregory later described the serpentine chasms and cracks as "enclosed" and "incised meanders." There are myriad options to hike, explore, and canyoneer these luminous Navajo Sandstone channels. But beware of flash floods that continue to sculpt these extraordinary canyons. Caused by winter rains, spring snowmelt in the headwaters of the Paria River, and summer monsoons, they are deadly. The author has day hiked, backpacked,

DRIVING AND HIKING ACCESS:

WHITE HOUSE TRAILHEAD AND CAMPGROUND:

From the Big Water Visitor Center, drive west 13.6 miles on U.S. Highway 89 to the turnoff for the White House Trailhead. Turn right onto the dirt road and drive 200 yards to the BLM Contact Station. The White House Trailhead and Campground is 2 miles beyond. White House hiking and canyoneering options include day hiking out and back from the campground 1.5 miles to The Windows, 4 miles to The Narrows, 6.5 miles to the confluence of Paria Canyon and Buckskin Gulch, or journeying through time 38 miles to Lees Ferry.

WIRE PASS TRAILHEAD:

From the Big Water Visitor Center, drive west 18.6 miles on U.S. Highway 89 to the House Rock Valley turnoff. Drive south on the House Rock Valley dirt road 8.3 miles to the Wire Pass Trailhead. From here, your options include day hiking out and back 1 to 3 miles through The Narrows, an overnight hike 21 miles to White House Trailhead, or embarking on an unforgettable canyon journey 44 miles one way to Lees Ferry.

LEES FERRY TRAILHEAD:

From the Navajo Bridge Interpretive Center, drive east on U.S. Highway 89A and immediately turn right on the paved Lees Ferry Road. Drive 4 miles to reach the Paria Canyon Trailhead at the Lonely Dell Ranch. Lees Ferry hiking and canyoneering options include day hiking out and back 1 mile to Lonely Dell Ranch, or hiking and backpacking as far upstream as the canyon calls you.

canyoneered, and run all of the options suggested in the Access sidebar, principally in the cloudless months of May, June, and October when the risk of deadly flash floods is minimized.

For complete details, visit: Vermilion Cliffs National Monument, www.blm.gov/az/st/en/arolrsmain/paria/trails.html

Earth Crack Adventure. PHOTO BY JOHN ANNERINO

Square Tower House. PHOTO BY JOHN ANNERINO

MESA VERDE NATIONAL PARK

Landscape, People, and Culture

Rising above the San Juan River between the shimmering reaches of the Painted Desert and the snowcapped San Juan Mountains, the 8,500-foot tablelands of Mesa Verde are crowned with forests of Douglas-fir, ponderosa pine, and piñon juniper. Ancestral Puebloans dwelled in the secret forests of deer, bear, and mountain lion, first in communal pit houses then later in 50 masonry pueblos, between AD 550 and 1200. Cleaved by 2,500-foot-deep canyons of Cretaceous sandstone, the overhanging alcoves beneath Wetherill and Chapin Mesas offered shelter for the ancient architects and skilled stonemasons who built 600 cliff dwellings, kivas, and towers during the height of their civilization. They used stone axes to cut hand- and footholds, today known as "Moqui steps," and hand-forged trails in the precipitous walls of 78-million-year-old Cliff House Sandstone to climb back and forth between their canyon homes and mesa farms. Using digging sticks, they farmed corn, beans, and squash to supplement wild game hunting. After 700 years, the forests, soil, and game were depleted, and the Ancestral Puebloans

Square Tower House. PHOTO BY NPS

left the area in AD 1300, leaving behind the most magnificent cliff dwellings in North America.

Geographically located in the heart of the Four Corners spiritual landscape, Mesa Verde is surrounded by many sacred landmarks. To the west, to name one, is Sleeping Ute Mountain. It was home to the Great Warrior God revered by the *Weminúcci,* "People Who Keep to the Old Ways," band of Southern Ute. To the east and south are the holy places of *Dibé nitsaa,* "Big Mountain Sheep," also known as Hesperus Peak, and *Tse' Bit' A'i,* "Rock with Wings," also known as Shiprock and revered by the Navajo throughout the ages. Ancestral traders and shamans used these hallowed mountains as landmarks during long-distance trading forays and pilgrimages before the coming of Spanish explorers and Mexican traders who traveled between Santa Fe, New Mexico, central Utah, and Mission San Gabriel, California. Pinched between the twin forks of the Old Spanish Trail, Mesa Verde was skirted to the north by the 1776 Dominguez–Escalante route and bypassed on the south by the 1829 Antonio Armijo route. As a result, Mesa Verde was rarely seen by outsiders until American photographer William Henry Jackson visited the cliff dwellings in the region he called *Mesa Verde,* "Green Tablelands." Attached to the 1874 U.S. Geological and Geographical

DRIVING ACCESS:

From Cortez, Colorado: Drive 9.9 miles east on U.S. Highway 160 to the Mesa Verde turnoff. Turn right on Mesa Verde 1, then turn left and drive a short distance to reach the Mesa Verde Visitor Center to purchase tickets required for visits to specific cliff dwellings. From the visitor center, drive 15 miles south on Mesa Verde 1 to the Far View Area road junction. Turn left on Chapin Mesa Road and drive 5 miles to the Chapin Mesa Archaeological Museum. The self-guiding 6-mile Cliff Palace Loop Road and 6-mile Mesa Top Loop Road described here begin nearby. To reach Wetherill Mesa from the Far View Area, turn right on Wetherill Mesa Road and drive 12 miles to the tram station.

Survey under Ferdinand V. Hayden, Jackson was the first known explorer to visit, enter, and photograph the cliff dwellings near Mesa Verde. In his 1876 report, "Ancient Ruins of Southwestern Colorado," Jackson described his perilous 500-foot evening ascent to Twin Story House in Mancos Canyon: "Soon we reached a slope, smooth and steep, in which there had been cut a series of steps . . . by which it was easy to ascend, and without them

Prairie rattlesnake. PHOTO BY NPS

an impossibility. . . . It was getting quite dark. . . . The house itself [was] perched in its little crevice like a swallow's nest."

Among these aeries were many other cliff dwellings and lost cities rediscovered and excavated by cowboy explorer Richard Wetherill, once described as the "American Southwest's greatest explorer—a 19th-century Indiana Jones." None was more impressive than the cliff dwelling that Wetherill's Ute guide Acowitz described to him: "One of those houses, high, high in the rocks, is bigger than all the others," Acowitz said. "Utes never go there. It is a sacred place." On December 18, 1888, Acowitz led Richard Wetherill and ranch hand Charles Mason into the hidden canyon where they dismounted their horses and climbed down rickety ladders to see one of the greatest cliff dwellings in the United States. Wetherill named it "Cliff Palace." Seeking to "preserve the works of man," President Theodore Roosevelt established Mesa Verde National Park on June 29, 1906. It is now recognized as a UNESCO World Heritage Site.

Ranger-guided tours of specific cliff dwellings require tickets purchased ahead of time at the Mesa Verde Visitor Center. Self-guided hiking is available on the 2.4-mile loop Spruce Canyon Trail, 2.4-mile loop Petroglyph Point Trail, and 1.2-mile out-and-back Soda Canyon Overlook Trail.

Scenic Roads and Views

Mesa Top Loop Road

- **Stop 1: Square Tower House Vista.** Square Tower House can be seen only from the rim of Echo Cliffs where Richard Wetherill and Charles Mason first viewed it before climbing down to the cliff dwellings on December 18, 1888.

Spruce Tree House. PHOTO BY NPS

Located in a shallow cave in Navajo Canyon, four-storied Square Tower House is 138 feet long. Its 49 rooms were home to about 100 Ancestral Puebloans who used eight ceremonial kivas. Unique among Mesa Verde's cliff dwellings is its 40-foot-tall Square Tower used as a lookout for defensive purposes.

Cliff Palace Loop Road

- **Stop 1: Cliff Palace Vista.** Cliff Palace is best seen from the opposite rim at Sun Point where Ute guide Acowitz first showed Richard Wetherill and Charles Mason the eagle's-eye view on December 18, 1888. Located in an immense cave at the head of Cliff Canyon, the multi-storied Cliff Palace is 300 feet long. Its 150 rooms were home to about 100 Ancestral Puebloans who used 23 ceremonial kivas. Unique among Mesa Verde's cliff dwellings is Cliff Palace's Round Tower, Square Tower, and "Speaker Chief's House." A ranger-guided 0.25-mile hike descends and climbs 100 feet each way.

- **Stop 2: Spruce Tree House.** Spruce Tree House is best viewed from the rim at the Chapin Mesa Museum where Richard Wetherill and Charles Mason first viewed it before climbing down to the cliff dwelling on December 18, 1888. Three-storied Spruce Tree House is 216 feet long. Its 130 rooms were home to about 80 Ancestral Puebloans who used eight kivas. A ranger-guided 0.5-mile hike descends and climbs 100 feet each way.

For additional park information, visit:

Mesa Verde National Park, www.nps.gov/meve

Moonrise over Cliff Palace. PHOTO BY JOHN ANNERINO

Tyúonyi with autumn colors. PHOTO BY SALLY KIING, NPS

BANDELIER NATIONAL MONUMENT

Landscape, People, and Culture

Located west of the Sangre de Cristo Mountains between the Caja del Rio Plateau and the Jemez Mountains, the 10,000-foot Pajarito Plateau drains into the upper Rio Grande through Frijoles, Alamo, and Capulin Canyons. Along their sterling creeks, with the volcanic cliffs and forested mesas above, Archaic hunters and gatherers roamed the primeval landscape in a never-ending quest for food, fire, and shelter. Between AD 1150 and 1550, Ancestral Puebloans built large pueblos, masonry houses, and kivas throughout the canyons and mesas of the Pajarito Plateau. Unique among their innovative architecture using natural materials were cliff-side cave dwellings called cavates. These "cave domiciles" were hand-carved and hollowed out in soft Bandelier Tuff that was deposited 1.4 million years ago when volcanic ash spewed from the magma chambers of the Valles Caldera during violent eruptions.

When Ancestral Puebloans deserted the Pajarito Plateau in AD 1600 and established river pueblos along the upper Rio Grande, it remained largely uninhabited until Captain Andrés Montoya was awarded the Rito de

DRIVING ACCESS:

From Santa Fe, New Mexico: Drive 16 miles north on U.S. Highway 84. Turn left on New Mexico Highway 502 and drive 11.7 miles west. Take the signed exit for Whiterock and Bandelier National Monument and continue south 12.6 miles on New Mexico Highway 4 to the monument entrance station. Continue 3.1 miles south to the visitor center.

Alcove House. PHOTO BY SALLY KING, NPS

Frijoles Land Grant by the Spanish Crown in 1740. Over the next century and a half, the grant changed hands with Montoya's descendants until 1883 when the U.S. Court of Private Land Claims, upheld by the U.S. Supreme Court, ruled that the land grant was invalid. Three years earlier, Cochití Pueblo elder Adelando Montoya invited Swiss-born ethnographer Adolph F. Bandelier to visit *Tyúonyi*, his ancestral home in Frijoles Canyon. Bandelier's repeated visits to the area with the Pueblo elder also led to a friendship with author, explorer, and former *Los Angeles Times'* city editor Charles F. Lummis. Bandelier's 1890 novel of cave dwellers in Frijoles Canyon, *The Delight Makers: A Novel of Pueblo Indian Life*, and Lummis' 1893 illustrated book, *The Land of Poco Tiempo*, drew attention to the little-known Pajarito Plateau and its people. Archaeologist, anthropologist, and author of the 1906 Antiquities Act, Edgar Lee Hewett surveyed the area between 1908 and 1911, describing it as "one of the wildest and most picturesque regions of the Southwest." On February 11, 1916, President Woodrow Wilson established 32,737-acre Bandelier National Monument.

Pueblo Walks into the Past

Main Loop Trail. From the visitor center, the self-guiding 1.2-mile trail leads in a counterclockwise direction to Big Kiva, Tyúonyi, Talus House, and Long House. Signed wooden ladders provide access to some of the cavates along the trail. Beyond Long House, a wooden footbridge crosses Frijoles Creek. At the trail junction there, you can turn left and follow the Nature Trail back to the visitor center or turn right and follow the 1-mile round-trip spur trail to Alcove House. Flooding and weathering sometimes close access to Alcove House; check at the visitor center for current conditions.

Highlights along the Main Loop Trail include:

- **Big Kiva.** Forty-two feet in diameter and 130 feet in circumference, the ceremonial kiva may have provided room for 50 to 60 Ancestral Puebloan singers, dancers, and participants during seasonal and spiritual observances.

- **Tyúonyi.** Constructed with hand-shaped blocks of Bandelier Tuff mortared together with mud, Tyúonyi was a

Tyúonyi and Talus House. PHOTO BY SALLY KING, NPS

Upper Frijoles Fall.
PHOTO BY SALLY KING, NPS

six-tiered high, circular pueblo with 242 rooms built around a central plaza that stretched 250 feet from the Rito de Frijoles to the opposite north wall of Frijoles Canyon.

■ **Talus House.** At one time, Talus House adjoining Long House stretched over a mile along the canyon wall and included 300 multi-storied cavates carved into the canyon walls and small pueblos built from Bandelier Tuff two to four terraces high.

■ **Long House.** In his book, *The Delight Makers*, Charles Lummis described how the two- and three-story caves were carved: "With their knives of chipped volcanic glass for sole tools, the Cochiteños builded [sic] their matchless village."

Juniper Campground. Located 2 miles from the visitor center, Juniper Campground offers 66 campsites in the pines with tent and parking pads, picnic tables, grills, and restrooms.

Tsankawi Section of Bandelier National Monument

Tsankawi Pueblo Village. This beautiful self-guiding 1.5-mile round-trip hike and scramble follows an Ancestral Puebloan trail deeply worn into the volcanic tuff. It leads to a spectacular "sky city" of pueblos, pictographs, and what archaeologist Edgar L. Hewett described as "the most picturesquely situated of any settlement of primitive people that I have ever seen." In Tewa, *Tsankawi* means "Place of the Round Cactus." The prehistoric settlement was comprised of four distinct, three-story-high pueblos. Its 200 rooms and 10 kivas supported 300 to 400 Ancestral Puebloans.

For further information, visit:
Bandelier National Monument, www.nps.gov/band/index.htm

DRIVING ACCESS:

The parking lot and trailhead for the Tsankawi Section of Bandelier National Monument is on the east side of New Mexico Highway 4 about 0.8 mile south of the interchange on New Mexico Highway 502, or about 100 yards north of the junction of NM 4 and East Jemez Road.

Cavates. PHOTO BY JOHN ANNERINO

Bisti formations. PHOTO BY JOHN ANNERINO

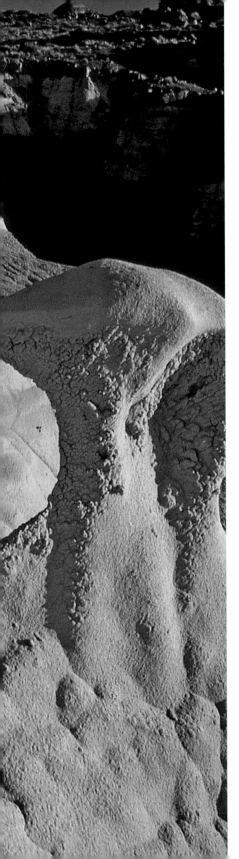

BISTI/
DE-NA-ZIN
WILDERNESS

Landscape, People, and Culture

All but lost in the empty sweep of the San Juan Basin between the ancient settlements of Aztec Ruins and Chaco Canyon, Bisti's captivating landscape is an anomaly of colors crossing the spectrum from monochromatic gray and coal black to cinnamon and buff. Many names were used to describe this barren, alien-looking "wasteland" on the edge of the Painted Desert. Spanish explorers and missionaries described such haunts in their expedition diaries as *Terra Incógnita,* "Unknown Land," *Mal País,* "Bad Country," and *Depoblado,* "Uninhabited Land." American cowboys and pioneers who traversed the forlorn Western deserts often cursed them as No Man's Land, Middle of Nowhere, and Badlands. Native Americans like the Navajo named the black rock desert after its landmark hoodoos, *Bistahí,* "Among the Adobe Formations." Beneath the surface of Bisti's mysterious caprocks, coal clinkers, and volcanic ash are the Cretaceous-aged Fruitland and Kirtland Formations—a prehistoric seashore of sand, shale, and mudstones—that revealed a wealth of oil, subbituminous coal, and, to paleontologists, a trove of fossilized trees, invertebrates,

Close-up of Bisti formation. PHOTO BY JOHN ANNERINO

fish, turtles, lizards, mammals, and dinosaur remains dating back 75 million years. During the "Bone Wars" between early American paleontologists, famed fossil collector Charles Hazelius Sternberg made one of the greatest discoveries of them all. In 1921, the field paleontologist unearthed a five-horned skull of a five-ton herbivorous dinosaur called a Pentaceratops. "Although it took many weary miles of travel," Sternberg wrote, "my best specimen, a Pentaceratops skull seven and one-half feet long, and the complete skeleton of a duckbilled dinosaur, were discovered in this formation." That was not the end of the dinosaur quest. In 1997, the meat-eating "Bisti Beast" was discovered by volunteer researcher Paul Sealey. News of the remains, now identified as a new tyrannosaur, *Bistahieversor sealeyi*, roared through the staid halls of academia and paleontology.

Centuries before America's "dinosaur gold rush," Ancestral Puebloans crossed the 5,980-foot-high desert that was too desolate and devoid of flora, fauna, wood, and water to sustain life. They surveyed and created ancient trails that followed a straight axis 55 miles north across the badlands, arroyos, and *quabradas*, or "broken country," between the thriving settlements of Chaco Canyon and Aztec Ruins. Recent studies suggest the 450-mile "Chaco Meridian" network of "roads" paralleling the Rio Grande on the west were built along the 108th Meridian and extended from Chaco 390 miles due south to the bustling Mesoamerican trade center of Paquimé in Chihuahua, Mexico.

DRIVING ACCESS:

From the junction of U.S. Highway 64 and New Mexico Highway 371 in Farmington: Drive 36.7 miles south on NM 371. Turn left on County Road 7295, a dirt road, and drive 2 miles to the junction with County Road 7290. Turn left and drive 1 mile on CR 7290 to the remote Bisti Wilderness pullout on the right. Camp carefully and with minimal impact. There are no facilities; bring your own water.

During the early 1870s, one small band of freed Navajo who survived the Long Walk and years of hunger, cold, and internment at Bosque Redondo had undoubtedly crossed Chaco's Great North Road when they entered the eastern Bisti Badlands and established a camp at Split Lip Flats. Tragically, they were attacked and decimated by a hostile band from another tribe not far from where pioneers later established a string of stores and trading posts linked by wagon roads that crisscrossed the Great North Road and Bisti's tributary washes. Among these was Swires trading store, started by two German immigrant brothers who operated out of an adobe and mud dwelling in 1878, trading goods and wool to Navajo sheepherders and weavers. It later became known as the Tiz Nat Zin Trading Post, a name derived from the Navajo description *Délí Náázíní*, "Standing Sandhill Cranes," for a nearby petroglyph of three cranes.

Operated by Winslow Wetherill, "the Black Sheep of the Wetherill family," from 1900 until 1902, the remote Tiz Nat Zin Trading Post changed hands many times by the time artist Georgia O'Keeffe first drove 150 miles of desolate back roads from her northern New Mexico Ghost Ranch in 1936 and discovered what she called the "Black Place." The famed "Mother of American Modernism"

returned to the Bisti Badlands many times over the course of the next 14 years where she camped, sometimes escaping the heat by sketching in the shade beneath her car. Here O'Keeffe found inspiration for her iconic oil paintings, *The Black Place, The Black Place II,* and *The Black Place III.* Her assistant Maria Chabot took a series of engaging black-and-white photographs of O'Keeffe standing against the black hills in her trademark wide-brimmed black parson's hat. Chabot, who started Santa Fe's Indian Market years earlier, wrote a letter to O'Keeffe's renowned husband, New York photographer Alfred Stieglitz, describing the scene of the August 1944 camping trip to Bisti Badlands: " . . . the black hills— black and grey and silver with arroyos of white sand curving around them—pink and white strata running through them. They flowed downward, one below the next.

Georgia O'Keeffe, the Black Place, 1944.
PHOTO BY MARIA CHABOT. PHOTOGRAPHIC PRINT, GIFT OF MARIA CHABOT (RC-2001-002-106B), © GEORGIA O'KEEFFE MUSEUM.

Incredible stillness!" Decades later, the hallucinatory landscape lured Academy Award-winning director William Friedkin to film the final scene of his 1977 thriller, *Sorcerer*, starring Roy Scheider of *Jaws* fame staggering through a South American jungle carrying a wooden box of unstable nitroglycerin to blow out a raging oil well fire. Who would have thought these secret badlands would have lured such a diverse array of visitors over the years.

Once known as the Fossil Forest Research Natural Area, the 3,968 Bisti Wilderness was established on October 30, 1984, along with the adjoining 23,983 De-Na-Zin Wilderness. The neighboring Ah-Shi-Sle-Pah Wilderness Study Area comprises 6,563 acres and can also be reached with intuitive orienteering skills.

Petrified tree. PHOTO BY USBLM, FARMINGTON FIELD OFFICE

Bisti landscape. PHOTO BY USBLM, FARMINGTON FIELD OFFICE

Your Journey of Discovery in *Bistahí*,
"Among the Adobe Formations."

In the tradition of Georgia O'Keeffe's independent, artistic explorations of Bisti Badlands, no paint-by-numbers route descriptions are provided to guide you through this wilderness which is managed to encourage no-impact, self-guided, walking-at-large. If Everett Ruess' "Leave No Trace" axiom should be followed to the letter anywhere in the 140,000-square-mile Colorado Plateau, it is here in this small, fragile area "Among the Adobe Formations." Get out of your vehicle and head into this dreamy and mystical landscape as far as you dare venture in whichever direction you're lured. Take care: The landscape is vulnerable and there are no trails; use natural direction finding, and take mental pictures of the subtle landmarks during your approach so you have a picture of the terrain for your return. Savor the evocative landforms, nature's handiwork, and the incomparable solitude and beauty.

Bisti hoodoos. PHOTO BY USBLM, FARMINGTON FIELD OFFICE

Hungo Pavi. PHOTO BY JOHN ANNERINO

CHACO CULTURE NATIONAL HISTORICAL PARK

Landscape, People, and Culture

Towering above the desolate 4,600-squaremile San Juan Basin are the forested heights of four principal ranges: the Chuska Mountains to the west and San Pedro Mountains to the east (both over 8,000 feet), the San Mateo Mountains rising higher than 11,000 feet to the south, and the San Juan Mountains (including 13,212-foot Hesperus Peak) far to the north. From these distant subalpine forests of ponderosa pine, spruce, fir, and aspen, Ancestral Puebloans felled and hand-carried 200,000 heavy timbers up to 60 miles across canyons, mesas, and badlands to Chaco Basin in order to build roofs over 12 multi-storied Great Houses and many small pueblos that formed the heart of Chaco Canyon civilization. These determined architects chiseled and shaped 75- to 80-million-year-old Cliff House Sandstone into masonry stones and then mortared them together with clay and mud to construct the walls of pueblos and kivas aligned with the sun, moon, and

Horned lizard with potsherd. PHOTO BY NPS

cosmos. The ancient engineers, astronomers, master stonemasons and their families hunted elk, mule deer, pronghorn, and bighorn sheep using atlatls and bows and arrows. Their diet was supplemented with plots of the Mesoamerican trinity of corn, beans, and squash tilled in gridded gardens with digging sticks and stone-tipped hoes. Nourished by water from seeps, springs, and rains, Chaco pueblos were built on or within reach of Chaco Wash, which was fed by runoff from the *rincons* and tributaries of Fajada, Cañada Alemita, Escavada, and Kimbeto Washes. Based on counts of pueblo and Great House rooms and fire pits, an estimated 13,544 people lived at Chaco Canyon between AD 850 and 1250. At its height, Chaco Canyon flourished as a sacred pilgrimage destination, ritual site, and trade center, where art, architecture, astronomy, and ceremony characterized the advanced civilization until drought, famine, and warfare precipitated its collapse.

Comprising 33,977.8 acres, Chaco Canyon National Monument was established by President Theodore Roosevelt on March 11, 1907. The national monument was designated Chaco Culture National Historical Park on December 19, 1980, and was later inscribed on the UNESCO World Heritage Site list on December 8, 1987.

Astronomers. Chaco Canyon's remote location and brilliantly clear night skies earned it a Gold-tiered Dark-Sky Park designation by the International Dark-Sky Association in August 2013.

Gallo Campground. Tucked between Gallo Wash and the cliffs of North Mesa, the undeveloped campground offers 49 campsites and 2 group sites with tent pads, picnic tables, grills, and two ADA-accessible restrooms. Casa de Alcove is clearly seen from the campground.

DRIVING ACCESS:

From Farmington, New Mexico: Drive west 12.6 miles on U.S. Highway 64 to County Road 550. Turn right and drive 36 miles on CR 550 to County Road 7950. Turn right on CR 7950 and follow the signs 24.3 miles to Chaco Canyon.

Chaco Canyon Scenic Drive

From Gallo Campground, drive the paved 1-mile scenic road to the visitor center at an elevation of 6,185 feet and the start of the Chaco Canyon Loop Road. En route, stop at the Fajada Butte Overlook on the left.

- **Stop 1: 6,623-foot Fajada Butte Overlook.** When Lieutenant James H. Simpson first rode horseback beneath the landmark butte on August 26, 1849, he wrote in his journal: "The chief object of the landscape was Mesa Fachada . . . the combination of this striking and beautiful object with the clear sky beyond . . . made up a picture which has seldom been my lot to address." *Fachada* is the Spanish name for an ornamental building "facade" that got lost in translation, misspelled *fajada*, and was later said to describe the sedimentary layers of Cliff House Sandstone that "wrap" around the butte. Sacred to many neighboring tribes, including the Hopi and Navajo, and Zuni, Acoma, Zia, and Santa Ana Pueblos, the 443-foot-tall butte is called *Sa'aktuyqa* by the Hopi. According to a Hopi elder, it was a holy place where "The Crier Chief . . . declared preordinations." For many years native peoples, shamans, and sun priests have traveled from the four directions to pay homage atop what the Navajo call *Tsé Diyil,* or "Sky Reaching Rock." Some still make the spiritual journey to the holy perch of golden eagles who nest where offerings of macaw feathers, turquoise, and shells were once made. Here lie the fragile remains of prayer shrines, astronomers' rooms, calendars, clan symbols, ceremonial minerals, and the remarkable "Sun Dagger." The spear shaft of solar light pierces a spiral petroglyph during the summer solstice, long ago marked by Hopi sun priests. Their ancestors, the *Hisat.sinom,* "People Who Lived Long Ago," may have also borne witness from here of the extraordinary supernova explosion in AD 1054. The event is depicted in a Chaco Canyon pictograph near Peñasco Blanco Pueblo. Fajada Butte and the traditional plant gathering area beneath its talus slopes are now closed to the public. The closure was brought about by visitor damage and unauthorized helicopter landings in the area revered by native peoples.

  Pueblos, Contemplative Walks, and Hikes. From the visitor center, the paved 9-mile loop drive runs counterclockwise through Chaco Canyon between 6,795-foot Chacra Mesa, 5,764-foot South Mesa, 6,449-foot North Mesa at Pueblo Alto, and 6,638-foot West Mesa. During the 1849 Navajo Expedition, Lieutenant James H. Simpson rediscovered, explored, and surveyed the pueblos throughout the 200-yard-wide *Cañon de Chaco* with his New Mexican guide Carravahal. The San Juan Pueblo native gave many of Chaco Canyon's landmarks and dwellings Spanish names that are still in use today.

■ **Stop 2: Una Vida Great House.** *Una Vida* is the Spanish name for "one life." The Navajo name *Asdzáá Halgóni Bikin* is said to mean "Place that Dries You Out."

Hike. A 1-mile round-trip hike from the visitor center leads to this Great House facing Fajada Butte. Una Vida pueblo includes 160 ground-floor rooms, four ceremonial kivas, and one great kiva in the southern corner of the plaza. Some researchers dispute the scientific gospel that circular archaeological remains are ceremonial kivas, but argue instead that many were ancient silos where precious staples of corn were stored as a hedge against drought and famine. Una Vida was first visited and sketched by Navajo Expedition artist Richard H. Kern, who also created 16 detailed floor plans of Chaco Canyon pueblos during the 1849 survey.

■ **Stop 3: Hungo Pavi Great House.** *Hongo Pavi* (or *Songòopavi*), "Reed Spring Village," is the Hopi name of the distant village on Second Mesa, Arizona. Located near the confluence of Mockingbird Canyon and Chaco Wash, Hungo Pavi pueblo includes 140 rooms, one ceremonial kiva, a great kiva in the southwest corner of the plaza, and hand-carved steps that lead up to the rim of North Mesa. When Southwestern Renaissance and travel writer Erna Fulton Fergusson visited Chaco Canyon in 1931, she recognized the strategic position of its pueblos. In her book, *Dancing Gods, Indian Ceremonials of New Mexico and Arizona*, she wrote, "Wherever the prehistoric Indian built, he always chose sites well defended by nature,

Hungo Pavi. PHOTO BY JOHN ANNERINO   *Walls, Chetro Ketl.* PHOTO BY JOHN ANNERINO

as were the cliff dwellings, or easily defended by man, as were the Chaco Canyon villages."

■ **Stop 4: Chetro Ketl Great House.** The origin of the name *Pueblo Chetho Kette* is not known but was interpreted to mean "Rain Pueblo" by guide Carravahal in 1849. The Navajo name *Tséjiitah* is said to mean "Inside Among Rocks." Chetro Ketl pueblo includes 400 rooms up to four stories high, two great kivas in the plaza, a colonnade, and a balcony. In her 1940 book, *Our Southwest*, Erna Fergusson lauded the canyon's fine masonry: "Chaco Canyon . . . was abandoned a hundred years or so before the Great Drought; yet its masonry is unsurpassed; it represents the highest stage that Pueblo culture ever reached."

■ **Stop 5: Pueblo Bonito Great House.** *Pueblo Bonito* is the Spanish name for "beautiful town." The Navajo name *Tsébiyaanii' áhá* is variously translated to mean "Leaning Rock Gap." Built in alignment with the four cardinal directions, Pueblo Bonito is Chaco's largest Great House and includes 350 rooms up to four stories high, 32 kivas, and 3 great kivas. A spur road off Chaco's Great North Road (see Bisti chapter) leads to the rim above Pueblo Bonito and linked the ritual center with pilgrims journeying from Aztec 60 miles north. First viewed by members of the 1849 Navajo Expedition on

Pueblo Bonito. PHOTO BY JOHN ANNERINO

August 28, Pueblo Bonito, later referred to as "downtown Chaco," became the center of interest for cowboy explorer Richard Wetherill. In a *Denver Magazine* feature, "Ghosts on the Mesa," Robert Sanchez wrote that Richard Wetherill "may have been the most influential American archaeologist of the late 19th century." Wetherill, with backing from the American Museum of Natural History, excavated 189 rooms at Pueblo Bonito between 1896 and 1900, homesteaded the 160-acre Section 12 in 1901, and operated the Pueblo Bonito trading post until he was ambushed with a .33 Winchester in 1910.

Wetherill Cemetery. Four Corners explorer, field archaeologist, and Quaker family man Richard Wetherill was buried in a humble cemetery beneath the walls of North Mesa after he was murdered by Chis-Chilling Begay on June 22, 1910. On the 100th anniversary of Wetherill's death, family members commemorated his Four Corners legacy at their great-grandfather's gravesite on his Pueblo Bonito homestead.

■ **Stop 6: Pueblo del Arroyo Great House.** *Pueblo del Arroyo* is the Spanish name for "village by the wash." The Navajo name *Tábaakiní* is said to mean "shore house" for its location next to Chaco Wash. Vulnerable to flash floods, the east-facing Pueblo del Arroyo includes 300 rooms up to four stories high and 17 kivas. In his 1930 book, *Ancient Life in the American Southwest*, archaeologist Edgar L. Hewett, who mapped Chaco Canyon, wrote tellingly of his profession: "We are now to challenge this realm of silence to give up its secrets. We are to clothe the bleaching bones of dead towns with new flesh and animate anew a race of men. If the archaeologist can not resurrect the sleeping past, cause the embers of ancient life to glow again, he has dug to no purpose."

Trails to Kin Kletso, Pueblo Alto, and Wetherill Cemetery. From Pueblo del Arroyo, a self-guiding 0.6-mile round-trip hike leads to the historic Wetherill Cemetery. Another popular self-guiding 0.6-mile round-trip hike leads to Kin Kletso. From Kin Kletso the 3.2-mile round-trip hike to Pueblo Alto gains 270 feet in elevation.

Pueblo Alto Great House. *Pueblo Alto* is the Spanish name for "village above," named by photographer William Henry Jackson, who, during the 1877 Hayden Survey, discovered it and the ancient hand-hewn stone stairway that climbed to it up the north wall. The Navajo name *Nihwiilbiih Bikin* is said to mean "Home of One Who Always Wins Them Over." Located atop 6,449-foot North Mesa on the Great North Road, the pilgrimage and ritual destination of Pueblo Alto includes 130 rooms and 18 kivas that offered eagle-eye views of Pueblo Bonito and line-of-sight communication with other Chaco Canyon pueblos. Scholar Frank Waters, author of the 1963 *Book of the Hopi*, studied the area and underscored the significance of Chaco's roads in Hopi spiritual beliefs in his paper, "The Race Tracks at Chaco Canyon:" "Chaco Canyon . . . contains the finest remains of an ancient civilization north of Mexico . . . . This great crossroads of all clans figures so prominently in the migration legends that we made two trips to Chaco Canyon, taking Hopi informants with us."

Return to Chaco Canyon Scenic Drive.

■ **Stop 7:** **Casa Rinconada Great Kiva.** *Casa Rinconada* is the Spanish name for "house in a corner." One of the Navajo names for the Great Kiva, *Kin Nahazbas* is said to mean "Circular House."

Hike. A graded 1-mile round-trip hike leads to this great kiva on an isolated rise located across the canyon from Pueblo Bonito. Casa Rinconada's Great Kiva is 63 feet in diameter, 12 to 15 feet deep, and includes a fire box, masonry benches, five adjoining rooms, an antechamber, and a hidden underground passage. Modern Hopi periodically return to the Great Kiva to celebrate and share the summer solstice sunrise ceremony.

Pueblo del Arroyo. PHOTO BY JOHN ANNERINO

Rimrock sandstone bluffs. PHOTO BY JOHN ANNERINO

EL MALPAIS AND EL MORRO NATIONAL MONUMENTS

EL MALPAIS NATIONAL MONUMENT

Landscape, People, and Culture

Imagine a molten river of lava created by earth-tremoring volcanic eruptions 3,900 years ago that created a hellish landscape of lava flows, craters, spatter cones, and cave tubes surrounded by supernal mountains, mesas, and deserts. That is El Malpais. A barrier to Spanish and Euro-American explorers, the glassy, knife-edged lava cut the hooves of horses and mules and the thick leather boots of unmounted riders, forcing conquistadors and pioneers to avoid the jagged belt of scoriaceous lava. For most, the best route was to give a wide berth around the angry landscape as they crested the Continental Divide between distant landmarks that stretched from the 11,000-foot San Mateo Mountains in the north to the high desert of the North Plains in the south, and from the 9,000-foot Zuni Mountains in the west to the Rio Puerco in the east. Ancestral Puebloans were the exception. Between AD 950 and 1350, sandal- and moccasin-clad travelers followed an ancient trade route 75 miles between the pueblos of Zuni and Acoma. Negotiating the bewildering course through the tortuous 170-square-mile lava flow, they marked the 7.5-mile "trail" by stacking three or four basalt rocks atop one another. They capped the charcoal-black cairns with easy-to-see buff-colored Zuni Sandstone. At first the treacherous terrain tested their balance and sure-footedness, evidenced by lithic scatters of broken pottery, arrowheads, and flint-knapped hide scrapers found along the primeval route. Over time, the 1,000-year-old trail and its branches became so familiar to them they used the rocky cinder paths to hunt elk, deer, and mountain lion and to gather pine nuts, juniper berries, and cactus fruit. They sometimes stored their reserves in ice caves and lava tubes near temporary one-room dwellings. In a landscape unimaginably harsh and unforgiving to most street-shoe-wearing visitors, the Ancestral Puebloans, Zuni, Acoma, Laguna, and Navajo made sacred pilgrimages to religious shrines among the ponderosa pine, piñon, and juniper on the lava flow. Today their descendants still revere the great lava flows as home of the Shalako and Katsina spirit beings, where traditional Navajo believe *Yé' iitso*, "Big God," spilled blood and created the obsidian-black lava.

In 1851, centuries after Ancestral Puebloans and Mogollon people left this hallowed ground, the Spanish Franciscan missionary priests Augustín Rodríquez and Francisco López crossed the country west of Santa Fe in quest of souls in the name of God as well as silver and gold for the Spanish Crown. But the friars got lost, or were ambushed, far from home in the heart of nowhere. News of their disappearance traveled south all the way to Mexico, where a valiant merchant and soldier named Don Antonio de Espejo launched an expedition to find the padres, only to discover during his epic journey they had been murdered. In his 1852-1853 expedition journal, diarist Diego Pérez de Luxán described and named the country that did not give up its secrets willingly: "March 7, [traveled] to Acomita; March 8, another four leagues past a marsh; March 9, another 4 leagues in waterless *malpais* [El Malpais]; March 10, 7 leagues, pine forest waterless mountain; March 11, three leagues, stopped

DRIVING ACCESS:

From Interstate 40 in Grants, New Mexico: Take Exit 89 (about 4 miles southeast of town) and drive 9 miles south on New Mexico Highway 117 to the El Malpais BLM Ranger Station.

at a water hole at the foot of a rock [El Morro]." Those who tried to follow the Spanish route across the old Zuni–Acoma trail discovered it was, indeed, *El Mal País*, "the bad country." Few tried, including Lieutenant James H. Simpson and the punitive 1849 Navajo Expedition. Returning from surveying Chaco Canyon, Simpson skirted El Malpais to the north and described the country on September 19: "A great deal of scoriaceous matter, in black angular fragments, lies scattered over the surface of this valley in piles and ridges."

Comprising 114,277 acres, El Malpais National Monument was established on December 31, 1987, by President Ronald Reagan. Adjoining the monument is the 263,000-acre El Malpais National Conservation Area, administered by the U.S. Bureau of Land Management.

Narrows Scenic Road

■ **Stop 1:** Sandstone Bluffs Overlook. From the BLM Ranger Station, drive 1 mile south on New Mexico Highway 117 and turn right onto the dirt Sandstone Bluff Road. Continue 1.5 miles to the parking area at road's end. From your car, it's a short scramble up to the ridgetop of Sandstone Bluffs. Use care walking and scrambling around the friable Dakota Sandstone that caps the Jurassic-aged Zuni Sandstone. The rims are exposed, with precipitous edges, drop offs, and *cañoncitos*, "little canyons," and are sometimes covered with slippery pebbles called "ball bearings." On the clear winter days the author visited the area, the horizon revealed the snow-covered

Sandstone Bluffs, El Malpais. PHOTO BY USBLM

San Mateo Mountains due north, home of *Yéi' iitso*, "Big God"; the spine of the Continental Divide tracing the crest of the Zuni Mountains to the northwest; and the sea of black lava threaded with the ancient footsteps and passages of Native peoples that stretched to the sunlit western horizon. Those same days, the *tinajas* and water pockets normally found here during summer monsoons and winter rains were frozen over with a thin veneer of ice that shined like gemstones against the coal-black lava below.

■ **Stop 2: Zuni-Acoma Trailhead.** The trailhead pullout is on NM 117, 6 miles south of the BLM Ranger Station. At 6,500 feet above sea level, don't underestimate this rugged 7.5-mile trail. It crosses a maze of ropy *pahoehoe* (pah-HOY-hoy) and sharp *a'a'* (AH-a) lava that requires care, fitness, and orienteering skills to reach the west-end trailhead on NM 53. Marked by basalt rock cairns, concrete posts, and blazes, the route makes use of pre-historic footbridges and offers wonderful glimpses of petroglyph panels to attentive eyes. The rock cairns were placed in the tradition of the Ancestral Puebloans who first "blazed" the trail. The concrete posts were installed to commemorate the area's Spanish legacy and 200-year anniversary of missionary explorers Francisco Atanasio Domínguez and Silvestre Vélez de Escalante. Dominguez and Escalante crossed the lava 15 miles north of this trail on November 14, 1776, and camped at a water hole named *Ojo del Gallo*, "Rooster's Eye," near San Rafael en route from El Morro to Acoma. The trail blazes mark a short leg of the 3,100-mile Continental Divide Trail. Many have found the "look-alike" terrain confusing. A father and daughter disappeared during an afternoon hike here in 2002, and their remains were not found for another eight years. Five other hikers have also disappeared. If you have any doubts, hike with more experienced companions, or do a short 1- or 2-mile round-trip hike to get a feel for the topography. Keep your eyes peeled for the next trail marker. Wear sturdy shoes, bring enough water, and avoid the area during hot summer months. Allow 5 to 7 hours: figure an average safe travel speed of 1 mile per hour through the lava flows.

■ **Stop 3: 8.6 miles, La Ventana Natural Arch.** The parking area, picnic area, and restrooms are on NM 117, on the east side of the road, 8.6 miles south of the BLM Ranger Station. The undeveloped 0.5-mile round-trip trail leads through talus, piñon, and juniper up to the base of La Ventana Natural Arch. Spanning 135 feet, New Mexico's second-largest arch has been weathered from 160-million-year-old Zuni Sandstone.

Zuni-Acoma Trail. PHOTO BY JOHN ANNERINO

El Malpais National Conservation Area Campground. Located 2 miles north of the BLM Ranger Station, the undeveloped campground offers 10 campsites, picnic tables, fire rings, shaded pavilions, and vault toilets. Bring your own water, which can be replenished at the ranger station.

For more information, visit:

El Malpais National Monument, National Park Service, www.nps.gov/elma/index.htm

El Malpais National Conservation Area, BLM, www.blm.gov/nm/st/en/prog/recreation/rio_puerco/el_malpais.html

EL MORRO NATIONAL MONUMENT
Landscape, People, and Culture

Located near the west end of the Zuni-Acoma Trail, El Morro shares much the same prehistory, Native American culture, and Spanish legacy as neighboring El Malpais. What distinguishes El Morro's 7,200-foot forested mesas and golden cliffs is the deep *tinaja*, "stone rain catchment," at the foot of the 200-foot, arrowhead-shaped point called *El Morro*, "The Promontory." On March 11, 1583, during his expedition's search for the missing Franciscan friars, Augustín Rodríquez and Francisco López, explorer Antonio de Espejo camped nearby and named the tinaja *El Estanque de Peñón*, "Tank at the Great Rock." Brimming with 200,000 gallons of snowmelt and rainwater, the tank nourished 1,500 Ancestral Puebloans who inhabited 875 multi-storied rooms on the mesa atop El Morro; their Zuni descendants called the mesa *A'ts'ina*, "Writing On the Rock." During the 75 years they inhabited the mesa between AD 1275 and 1350, they were among the first to carve symbols of their culture in the 150- to 200-million-year-old Zuni Sandstone that included bighorn sheep, handprints, and more abstract depictions. Among the more than 2,000 inscriptions and petroglyphs recorded on the sheer, iron oxide–streaked walls is that of explorer, colonizer, and New Mexico governor Don Juan Oñate, who wrote: *Paso por aq[u]i el adelantado Don Ju[an] de Onate del descubrimyento de la mar del sur a 16 de Abril de 1605.* "Don Juan de Onate passed through here, from the discovery of the Sea of the South [Pacific Ocean] on the 16th of April, 1605."

DRIVING ACCESS:
From Interstate 40 in Grants, New Mexico: Turn onto New Mexico Highway 53 and drive 42 miles south and west to El Morro National Monument Visitor Center.

Oñate's historic inscription was one of the first records of Spanish explorations during their ruthless campaigns against the neighboring pueblo peoples at Zuni and Acoma. But author Charles F. Lummis' September 1, 1926, visitor register entry is perhaps the most telling of El Morro's rich history of inscriptions: "No other cliff on earth records a time as much of romance, adventure, heroism. Certainly all the other rocks in America do not, all together, hold so much of American history. Oñate here carved his entry with his dagger two years before an English speaking person had built a hut anywhere in the New World, and 15 years before Plymouth Rock. The Point, El Morro."

Comprising 1,278 acres, President Theodore Roosevelt established El Morro National Monument on December 8, 1906.

Inscription Trail. The paved ADA-accessible 0.5-mile loop trail leads to *El Estanque de Peñón*, "Tank at the Great Rock," in a corner of El Morro. When full, El Estanque holds 200,000 gallons of water, almost ten times the 21,500 gallons of water that *Tinajas Altas*, "High Tanks," offered travelers on the deadly *Camino del Diablo*, "Road of the Devil" through Arizona and Sonora, Mexico. Take your time to study the myriad petroglyphs at the foot of the beautiful walls leading from this oasis in the pines. Missing from the Spanish inscriptions are those of Antonio de Espejo, who camped here in 1583, and Domínguez and Escalante, who camped here on November 14, 1776. It's easy to imagine the weary conquistadors and their mounts slaking their thirst with the cool, sweet water from the same natural trough where Ancestral Puebloans filled their ollas to haul up to their cook fires atop the spectacular cliffs at A'ts'ina.

El Morro Campground. Located in a stand of fine ponderosa pines, the campground offers nine campsites on a first-come, first-served basis that include picnic tables, fire rings, drinking water, and restrooms.

For more information, visit:
www.nps.gov/elmo/index.htm

Inscription rock. PHOTO BY JOHN ANNERINO

Temple of the Moon. PHOTO BY JOHN ANNERINO

CAPITOL REEF NATIONAL PARK

Landscape, People, and Culture

Saddled between 11,316-foot Boulder Mountain in the west and the 11,000-foot Henry Mountains in the east, the 7,000-foot-high Waterpocket Fold cuts across the high desert from the Fremont River 100 miles south to the Colorado River in Glen Canyon. Over 200 million years of geological history is exposed in the Waterpocket Fold's dramatic landscape. Its colorful landmarks include the Wingate Sandstone spires of the Castle, the Navajo Sandstone swells and chasms of Navajo Dome and Grand Wash narrows, the Entrada Sandstone pyramids of Temples of the Sun and Moon, and the shale and mudstone desert of the Mancos Badlands. During an uplift of the Colorado Plateau 60 million years ago, the earth buckled then folded, creating a 0.5-mile-high monocline of serrated fins, ridges, and deep narrow valleys that resemble rows of fossilized shark's teeth. Paleontologists recovered marine fossils in the 720-million-year-old Tunupk Member of Mancos Shale. For early travelers, the titanic reef and troughs looked like an insurmountable barrier, but the ancient Fremont people traced sinuous canyons through what the

Paiute later called *Timpiavic,* "Rock Mountain." North to south the east-trending chasms included Fremont River Gorge, Grand Wash, Capitol Gorge, and Muley Twist Canyon, among others used by the Fremont people between AD 700 and 1250. Wearing deerskin moccasins, they trod through the narrow corridors between seasonal hunting and gathering camps and hand-tilled plots of corn, beans, and squash.

The first Euro-American explorers to literally follow their footprints across the imposing reef was the 1872 Powell Survey. Led by explorer and geologist Almon Harris Thompson, the nine-man expedition set out to map the uncharted wilderness between Boulder Mountain, the Henry Mountains they called the "Unknown Mountains," and the Colorado River. Their goal was to recover the *Cañonita,* a boat Major John Wesley Powell had cached at the mouth of the Dirty Devil River the year before, and row it 154 miles down the Colorado River through Glen Canyon to Lees Ferry. Searching for a route across the fold near Pleasant Creek and Tantalus Flat, expedition photographer John K. Hillers noticed the campfire smoke of an Indian camp one night. The next morning the expedition pow-wowed with a group of Red Lake Utes, and

Sunset, The Castle. PHOTO BY JOHN ANNERINO

DRIVING ACCESS:

From the junction of Utah Highways 12 and 24 in Torrey, Utah:
Drive 11.8 miles east on UT 24 to the visitor center on the right.

Temple of the Sun. PHOTO BY JOHN ANNERINO

the chief gave them directions through the spine of rock. On June 13, expedition member Frederick Dellenbaugh wrote, "The chief gave us a minute description of the trail to the Unknown or Dirty Devil Mountains as well as he could by signs and words, some of which we could not understand, and long afterwards we learned that this information was exactly correct." The Pleasant Creek area later became the site of the "Mormon underground railroad," where settler Eph Hanks harbored "cohabs," polygamists on the run from U.S. marshals enforcing the 1882 Edmunds Act. Among those who also brought life and legend to what the Navajo were said to call "The Land of the Living Rainbow," were surveyors, Mormon pioneers, cowboys, and the lawmen who tracked horse thieves, bank robbers, and moonshiners through Capitol Reef's maze of canyons.

President Franklin D. Roosevelt established 37,711-acre Capitol Reef National Monument on August 2, 1937. Now comprising 242,000 acres, it was designated Capitol Reef National Park by President Richard M. Nixon on December 18, 1971.

Capitol Reef Scenic Drive

From the visitor center, the paved scenic drive leads 10.5 miles south along the western cliffs of the Waterpocket Fold over the Slickrock Divide to Capitol Gorge. The scenic drive follows the historic wagon road settler Elijah Cutler

Fruita and Wingate Cliffs. PHOTO BY JOHN ANNERINO

Behunin and his crew built in 1883 to link Fruita with the distant settlements of Notom and Hanksville via Capitol Gorge.

■ **Stop 1: 1.0 mile, Fruita Historic District, on right.** Near the confluence of the Fremont River and Sulphur Springs, Mormon pioneers Nels Johnson, Leo Holt, and brothers Hyrum and Elijah Cutler Behunin homesteaded 200 acres in the small verdant valley in 1886. They built log cabins, a one-room schoolhouse, barns, root cellars, and a blacksmith shop. They also dug irrigation ditches to nurture peach, apricot, and apple orchards and crops that included potatoes, squash, and corn. By 1910, the self-sufficient population of the isolated community at the foot of Wingate Sandstone cliffs had grown to 61 men, women, and children. Today, a self-guiding tour leads through Fruita, a model of pioneer life on the harsh frontier.

■ **Stop 2: 1.25 miles, Fruita Campground, on right.** Called an "oasis in the desert," the Fruita Campground offers 71 tent/RV sites with picnic tables, grills, drinking water, and restrooms.

■ **Stop 3: 3.4 miles, Grand Wash, on left.** Turn left onto the dirt road and drive 1.3 miles to the trailhead at road's end. En route you'll see the portals of the Oyler Mine, a now-abandoned uranium mine, and the Cassidy Arch Trailhead on the left. From the Grand Wash Trailhead, the easy 2.25-mile Grand Wash Trail leads beneath slickrock walls of Navajo Sandstone, eventually arriving at UT 24 about 4.5 miles east of the Capitol Reef Visitor Center. The canyon passageway was once used by cowboys to drive cattle between summer pastures in the Waterpocket Fold and winter ranges in the South Desert. The area was said to be used by moonshiners who operated a still near Cassidy Arch and made whiskey and brandy distilled from corn and grapes grown in Fruita.

Return to the Scenic Drive.

Canyon wren. PHOTO BY SARAH STIO, NPS

Desert spiny lizard. PHOTO BY MICHAEL QUINN, NPS

- **Stop 4: 8.4 miles, Slickrock Divide.** At 5,980 feet, this scenic high point offers good views of the piñon, juniper, and turbinella oak-covered landscape and western escarpment of the Waterpocket Fold.

- **Stop 5: 10.5 miles, Capitol Gorge, on left.** Turn left into the Capitol Gorge Picnic Area, where the pavement ends. From here you can view a pointed Wingate Sandstone peak on the southern rim. Named Eph Hanks Tower after the Fruita pioneer, the 6,540-foot tower can be reached from the picnic area via a rugged, self-guiding cross-country route, and a 1,000-vertical-foot scramble and exposed climb up the easiest approach to the summit.

  From the picnic area, drive on the dirt road another 2.3 miles east to the Capitol Gorge Trailhead. The road and easy foot trail form what was once part of the "Blue Dugway" that led from Fruita to the settlements of Notom and Hanksville before UT 24 was built and rerouted through Fremont River Gorge. Fruita founder Elijah Cutler Behunin and community members forged the road through the flash-flood-swept Capitol Gorge during an arduous eight-day period in 1883. From the Capitol Gorge Trailhead, the easy 0.8-mile trail leads to the Tanks formation and offers views of the Golden Throne and "pioneer registers" that were pecked and chiseled into the Navajo Sandstone walls of the canyon. Others used this route as well. Traveling between his home in Circle Valley and their hideout at Robbers Roost in the San Rafael Swell, Butch Cassidy and the Wild Bunch rode hell-for-leather through Capitol Gorge to cross the Waterpocket Fold during the 1880s-1890s. Born to a devout Mormon family of 14, Robert Leroy Parker, aka "Butch Cassidy," and his sidekick Harry Longabaugh, aka the "Sundance Kid," and their partners in crime formed the Wild Bunch, one of the most notorious gangs in the West. Utahns did not always frown on their bank robberies and holdups that drew the attention of Pinkerton detectives because Butch was said to live by a Robin Hood code: "The best way to hurt them is through their pocket book . . . I steal their money just to hear them holler. Then I pass it out among those who really need it."

Return to the visitor center.

Hickman Natural Bridge Hike

This rugged 1-mile hike entails a 400-foot vertical climb that zigzags up loose ledges of Kayenta Sandstone to Hickman Natural Bridge. The ancient path was no doubt pioneered by Fremont people and later used by Ute, and also by local moonshiners who relied on clean spring water at nearby Whiskey

Springs. Comprised of Navajo Sandstone, Hickman Natural Bridge stands 125 feet above the canyon arroyos, and its 25-foot-thick truss spans 133 feet. It was named in honor of Joseph S. Hickman, who spearheaded the movement during the 1920s to get Capitol Reef, located in Wayne County, established as Wayne Wonderland. But Hickman drowned in Fish Lake days after introducing legislation in 1925. His brother-in-law, Ephraim Pectol, was later known as the "father of Capitol Reef," because he carried the torch for the next 12 years when he asked Congress to establish Wayne Wonderland National Monument. On the descent back to the trailhead, look south across Fremont River Gorge to see the spectacular landmark of 6,526-foot Pectol's Pyramid, named in honor of the state legislator and Mormon elder.

For more information, visit: www.nps.gov/care/index.htm

HIKING ACCESS:

From the Capitol Reef National Park Visitor Center: Drive 1.9 miles east on UT 24 to the Hickman Bridge Trailhead parking area on the left. On the way, 1 mile from the visitor center on UT 24, watch for the scenic stop and short walk on the left to view Fremont era (AD 700 to 1250) petroglyphs of shamans and dancers chiseled into the Wingate Sandstone walls of Fremont Gorge.

Hickman Bridge. PHOTO BY NPS

Bryce hoodoos. PHOTO BY JOHN ANNERINO

BRYCE CANYON NATIONAL PARK

Landscape, People, and Culture

Located in the High Plateaus of Utah and Arizona, the 56-square-mile Paunsaugunt Plateau was formed during an ancient uplift of the Colorado Plateau. The region-wide uplift and fault fracturing created a sublime tableland-in-the-sky 9,105 feet high, 28 miles long, and 6 to 15 miles wide. Crowned with relic stands of ancient bristle-cone pine, forests of blue spruce, white fir, and yellow pine, aspen groves, and alpine meadows, the spectacular landmass receives on average 200 inches of snow a year. Abundant runoff tumbles into the East Fork of the Sevier River on the west and the Paria River on the east. Through seasonal freeze-thaw erosion, oxidation, and the chemical reaction of water dissolving the silt and mudstone of the Eocene-aged Clarion Formation, extraordinary landmarks have been sculpted along the narrow 35-mile-long southeastern ramparts of the Paunsaugunt Plateau. The 1871-1872 Powell Survey called these the "Pink Cliffs," where today peregrine falcons and visitors alike peer from rim tops into 14 luminescent

1,000-foot-deep bays and amphitheaters. "Fairylands" of fins, hoodoos, windows, natural bridges, and canyon arroyos display 60 distinct shades of color between sunrise and sunset. Known as *Paunsaganti*, "Beaver Place," by the Kaibab band of Southern Paiute, these forests, brooks, creeks, and desert lowlands were home to elk, mule deer, mountain lion, black bear, pronghorn, bighorn sheep, and rabbits. The land also produced a nutritional cornucopia of edible nuts, berries, grasses, flowers, and medicinal plants that ancient peoples depended on. Cold weather and heavy, deep snowpack discouraged permanent settlement on the high plateau. Ancient nomads, who the Paiute called the *Mukwic*, or "Those We Never Saw," and, later, Kaibab Paiute, passed through on seasonal journeys to hunt, gather, and till small plots of corn.

The first to record the geological marvels of the Pink Cliffs were members of the 1871–1872 Powell Survey. Under the direction of Major John Wesley Powell, they explored the High Plateaus between Kanab, Utah, and the Dirty Devil River, crossing the spine of Capitol Reef en route. Expedition artist Frederick S. Dellenbaugh described the striking scenery that greets most visitors today: "Emerging from the forest of pine and cedar we saw again the magnificent, kaleidoscopic, cliff country lying to the north . . . . A more extraordinary, bewildering landscape, both as to form and colour, could hardly be found in all the world." Mormon pioneers, sheepherders, and cowboys riding herd for the Canaan Cooperative Stock Company were more interested in wresting a living from beautiful scenery that could be marketed, prepared, cooked, and eaten. Among them was Scottish immigrant Ebenezer Bryce, his wife Mary Ann Park, and their family of twelve children who lived in a hand-hewn log cabin in 1875. The couple homesteaded 200 acres in Tropic, Utah, at the mouth of what locals called "Bryce Canyon." Water in the arid landscape at the foot of the Pink Cliffs was scarce for cattle, sheep, and farming. So Bryce and his hardy neighbors spent three years digging a 15-mile trench called the Tropic Ditch from the East Fork of the Sevier River up over the rim of the Paunsaugunt Plateau to their homesteads near the forest of hoodoos that Ebeneezer famously said were "A hell of a place to lose a cow." The Scottish shipbuilder put his considerable skills into building logging roads, log cabins, water diversion projects, and

DRIVING ACCESS:

From Kanab, Utah: Drive 61.1 miles north on U.S. Highway 89 to the turnoff for Utah Highway 12. Turn right on UT 12 and drive 13.5 miles through Red Canyon to the turnoff for Utah Highway 63. Turn right on UT 63 and drive 3.7 miles to the visitor center.

the historic Pine Valley Chapel, modeled after a wooden ship. But the harsh elements finally won out. In 1880 Ebenezer packed his family and belongings in a wooden wagon and drove south on iron rims 569 miles down the Mormon Trail to Arizona, where he homesteaded a family ranch near Pima. The small community of Bryce, Arizona, is just across the Gila River from Pima. Ebenezer was later buried next to his wife in the Ashurst Cemetery far from the bustling national park named in his honor.

Now comprising 35,835 acres, Bryce Canyon National Monument was established by President Warren G. Harding on June 8, 1923. Under President John Calvin Coolidge, Congress passed legislation to rename the monument Bryce Canyon National Park on February 25, 1928.

North Campground. Located near the general store, North Campground offers 13 RV sites available by reservation and 86 tent/RV sites on a first-come, first-served basis in ponderosa pines with picnic tables, fire grills, restrooms, and drinking water.

Bryce hoodoos close-up. PHOTO BY JOHN ANNERINO

Sunset Campground. Located near Sunset Point, Sunset Campground offers 20 tent sites and a group site available by reservation, and 80 tent/RV sites on a first-come, first-served basis in ponderosa pines with picnic tables, fire grills, restrooms, and drinking water.

Bryce Canyon Scenic Drive

From the visitor center the 16-mile paved scenic drive leads south along the rim of the Paunsaugunt Plateau's Pink Cliffs to 9,115-foot Rainbow Point. To reach Fairyland Point from the visitor center, drive 1 mile *north* to the signed turnoff, turn right, and follow the signs 1 mile to Fairyland Point.

■ **Fairyland Point.** From the 7,758-foot vista overlooking Fairyland Canyon and Boat Mesa, you can gaze northeast and see the rugged, uncharted terrain the 1871–1872 Powell Survey traversed en route to the Dirty Devil River, including the 10,158-foot Table Cliff Plateau and the distant Aquarius Plateau. What will steal your attention, though, are the intimate three-dimensional views of hoodoos that, to early Paiute, resembled totems of people who were turned to stone in the steep, arid forest of Douglas-fir, piñon, and juniper.

Thor's Hammer. PHOTO BY NPS

Hikes. From Fairyland Point, the spectacular 5.5-mile Rim Trail leads south to Sunrise, Sunset, Inspiration, and Bryce Points. For starters, walk the easy Rim Trail 2.5 miles south to Sunrise Point. (The other points can also be viewed from the scenic drive.)

Return to the visitor center turnoff and resume driving south on the Bryce Canyon Scenic Drive.

- **Stop 1: 0.5 mile from the visitor center.** Sunrise Point turnoff. Follow the signs to 8,015-foot Sunrise Point, overlooking the Sinking Ship and Bryce Canyon. This is the first vista stop on the 5.5-mile Rim Trail from Fairyland Point to Bryce Point.

  Hikes. The moderate rim-to-canyon Queens Garden Trail is 1.8 miles round-trip and descends and climbs 320 vertical feet in each direction. Beginning at Sunrise or nearby Sunset Point, the park's most popular hike is the 2.9-mile Queens Garden/Navajo Loop Trail that offers up-close views of Queens Garden, Queen Victoria, Thor's Hammer, The Sentinel, and the towering Douglas-fir tree of Wall Street.

- **Stop 2: 1.2 miles from the visitor center.** Sunset Point turnoff. Follow the signs to 7,999-foot Sunset Point overlooking Bryce Amphitheater and an amazing array of hoodoos. At sunset, busloads of visitors disembark here with cameras at the ready. This is the second vista stop on the 5.5-mile Rim Trail from Fairyland Point to Bryce Point.

- **Stop 3: 1.7 miles, Bryce Point Road; Inspiration Point turnoff.** From this turnoff, turn left and follow the signs 1 mile to 8,143-foot Inspiration Point overlooking Bryce Amphitheater. This is the third vista stop on the 5.5-mile Rim Trail from Fairyland Point to Bryce Point. Imagine building a wagon road up Bryce Canyon with picks, shovels, and pry bars, sawing heavy timber, and hauling the unwieldy logs down to the town site of Tropic to build a rudimentary cabin for your family, as Ebenezer Bryce did.

- **Stop 4: Bryce Point.** From Inspiration Point, return to Bryce Point Road (not the main Bryce Canyon Scenic Drive), turn left and drive 1.2 miles south to a fork in the road. Follow signs left 0.6 mile to 8,294-foot Bryce Point overlooking Bryce Amphitheater. This is the fourth and last vista stop on the 5.5-mile Rim Trail from Fairyland Point to Bryce Point. Bryce Point offers colorful sunrise views of the 7,040-foot Kaiparowits Plateau to the east and sunset views of Wall of Windows to the west.

  Hikes. The strenuous 11.5-mile Under-the-Rim Trail begins or ends here and leads south to 9,105-foot Rainbow Point.

Bryce Canyon. PHOTO BY NPS

- **Stop 5: Paria View.** From Bryce Point, return to the fork in the road and stay right, following signs 0.4 mile to 8,176-foot Paria View overlooking the Pink Cliffs. Working under the direction of Major John Wesley Powell and the U.S. Geological Survey, eminent geologist Clarence E. Dutton surveyed and published the 1880 *Report on the Geology of the High Plateaus of Utah.* Dutton had a flair for colorful descriptions of the landmarks of the Grand Canyon and Colorado Plateau, including the hoodoos of the Pink Cliffs: "Standing obelisks, prostrate columns, shattered capitals . . . all bring vividly before the mind suggestions of the work of giant hands, a race of genii now chained up in a spell of enchantment, while their structures are falling in ruins through centuries of decay."

Return to Bryce Canyon Scenic Drive.

Turn left and continue south on Bryce Canyon Scenic Drive 14 miles to 9,115-foot Rainbow Point. On this spectacular high point of the Paunsaugunt Plateau, ancient bristlecone pines cling to life at land's end. Views north from Rainbow Point encompass much of the park's colorful cliffs and canyons. Walk south about 200 yards from the parking lot to Yovimpa Point for a vista of the Grand Staircase revealed in descending order from the Pink Cliffs to the White Cliffs, and finally the Vermilion Cliffs in the far distance.

For further information, visit: www.nps.gov/brca/index.htm

Bryce hoodoos. PHOTO BY JOHN ANNERINO

Virgin River Narrows. PHOTO BY JOHN ANNERINO

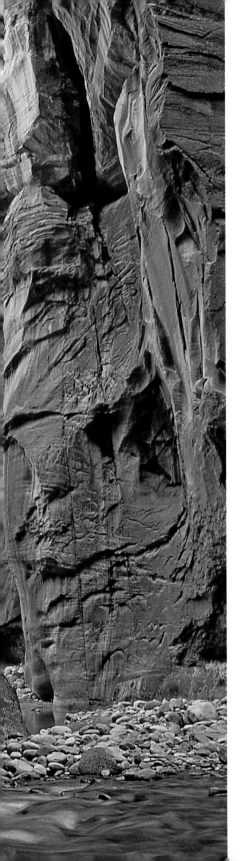

ZION NATIONAL PARK

Landscape, People, and Culture

A bold and beautiful landscape on the western edge of the Colorado Plateau, Zion is surrounded by high plateaus, inland seas of sand, caprock, and deep canyons that characterize much of the arid West. Great stone temples, forested terraces, and lush canyons intermingle with sandy flats, sun-scorched badlands, and dry piñon–covered mesas, creating a storybook landscape sculpted by the hands of nature for 240 million years. A 2,200-foot layer of fossilized sand dunes named for indigenous people, the Jurassic-aged Navajo Sandstone has been carved by wind, water, and freeze-thaw erosion on a scale found nowhere else in North America. These natural processes created cathedrals of stone, narrow chasms, and cliff ledges of such beauty and mystery they were named for Old Testament figures, Native American gods, and heavenly angels.

As a sanctuary for flora and fauna, Zion boasts a rich biodiversity, due in part to the park's wide elevational range, from the 8,933-foot heights of Kolob Terrace to the flash-flood-scoured depths of the Virgin River at 3,747 feet in the Mojave Desert lowlands. Here elk and mule deer, mountain lions and bobcats, peregrine falcons and ravens, aspens and cottonwoods, and maidenhair ferns and columbine flowers still thrive where Archaic hunters once brought down bellowing mastodons with hand-thrown spears called atlatls. Ancestral Puebloans later hunted deer, pronghorn, and rabbits with bows and arrows, tilling small plots of corn they harvested and stored in hand-painted pots. The Southern Paiute also found a home among the spectacular cliffs, canyons, and verdant valleys that remained hidden from Spanish missionaries Domínguez and Escalante, mountain man Jedediah Strong Smith, and other early explorers who skirted the supernal sandstone towers and domes. That changed in 1858 when the Paiute guide Nauguts led Mormon missionary Nephi Johnson to Zion Canyon, where farmers and ranchers soon established the settlement of Shunesburg. A decade later, Major John Wesley Powell was, in turn, guided into Zion by Mormon missionary explorer Jacob V. Hamblin. Theirs was the first known party to "canyoneer" Zion's frigid canyon narrows. In Powell's 1870 report, *Exploration of the Colorado River of the West,* the one-armed father of American canyoneering wrote, "In some places the holes are so deep that we have to swim, and our little bundles of blankets and rations are fixed to a raft of driftwood . . . we cross and recross the stream, and wade along the channel where the water is so swift as to almost carry us off our feet . . . we are in danger every moment of being swept down, until night comes." Having survived their audacious first-recorded descent down the East Fork of the Virgin River, which the Paiute called *Pa-rú-nu-weap,* or "Roaring Water Canyon," Hamblin and Powell traveled north through the green

DRIVING ACCESS:

From St. George, Utah: Drive north 7 miles on Interstate 15, take Exit 16, and drive 12.2 miles east on Utah Highway 9, following signs for UT 9 through the town of Hurricane and north into La Verkin. Turn right on West 500 North and continue on Utah Highway 59 east another 20.5 miles to the park entrance in Springdale. The Zion Canyon Visitor Center is on the right.

From Kanab, Utah: Drive 17.1 miles north on U.S. Highway 89 to Mount Carmel Junction. (It's well worth stopping in the hamlet of Mount Carmel to visit the historic home and art gallery of Western painter Maynard Dixon.) Turn left onto Utah Highway 9 and drive 21.1 miles west on the Zion-Mount Carmel Highway, past Checkerboard Mesa and through the tunnels and switchbacks to Zion Canyon Scenic Drive. Turn left and drive 1.1 miles south to the Zion Canyon Visitor Center on the left.

valley of Zion Canyon on September 12, 1870, and entered the North Fork of the Virgin River, which, Powell learned, the Paiute called *Mu-koon-tu-weap*, or "Straight Canyon."

Recognizing the cultural legacy of Native Americans in this great western landscape, President William Howard Taft established Mukuntuweap National Monument on July 31, 1909. Now comprising 146,598 acres—nearly 600 square miles—President Woodrow Wilson established Zion National Park on November 20, 1919.

Watchman Campground. Located 0.5 mile from the South Entrance Station on the Virgin River below the landmark 6,545-foot Watchman, the campground offers 171 campsites by reservation. Facilities include picnic tables, fire grates, and restrooms. Visit www.recreation.gov.

Zion shuttle bus. PHOTO BY NPS

South Campground. Located 0.5 mile from the South Entrance Station on the Virgin River near the Watchman, the South Campground offers 127 campsites on a first-come, first-served basis that include picnic tables, fire grates, and restrooms.

Zion Canyon Scenic Drive Shuttle. The paved Zion Canyon Scenic Drive leads from the visitor center 7.1 miles north to the trailhead at Zion Canyon Narrows. Between April and October, private vehicles are not allowed on Zion Canyon Scenic Drive. But the free Zion Canyon Loop shuttle stops at nine popular roadside points of interest and trailheads in between. Parking lots inside Zion often fill by mid-morning. Use the free town shuttles that run between Springdale and Zion Canyon Visitor Center. All shuttles are air-conditioned. Within the park, shuttles run frequently, as often as every seven minutes during peak times, so waits are never long.

For the shuttle schedule, visit: www.nps.gov/zion/planyourvisit/shuttle-system.htm

Zion Canyon Scenic Drive Scenic Vistas and Stops

- **Towers of the Virgin:** 6,364-foot Three Marys, 7,810-foot West Temple, 7,438-foot Sun Dial, and 7,410-foot Altar of Sacrifice, located behind the Human History Museum.

- **Court of the Patriarchs:** 6,990-foot Abraham, 6,825-foot Isaac, 6,831-foot Jacob, and 5,690-foot Mount Moroni, named after figures from the *Bible* and *Book of Mormon* by 16-year-old Claud Hirschi in 1916.

- **Great White Throne:** 6,744-foot Great White Throne, named by Methodist minister Frederick Vining Fisher in 1916.

- **Temple of Sinawava:** 4,418-foot Temple of Sinawava, located at the mouth of Virgin River Narrows.

Angels Landing Hike

This knife-edged fin of pink and white Navajo Sandstone towers 1,488-feet above the floor of Zion Canyon. When photographer John K. Hillers first took a stereographic picture of 5,790-foot Angels Landing for the U.S. Geological Survey in 1872, he called it Temple of Aeolus for the man-made temple Sir William Chambers built atop Cumberland Mount in London's Kews Garden in 1763 in honor of the mythic Greek god of wind. Built with picks, shovels, pry bars, and black powder in 1926, the 2.5-mile Angels Landing Trail leads from

Towers of the Virgin. PHOTO BY JOHN ANNERINO

HIKING ACCESS:

Take the park shuttle to the West Rim Trail–Angels Landing Trailhead at The Grotto on Zion Canyon Scenic Drive.

the West Rim Trail and climbs 21 steep, narrow switchbacks called Walters Wiggles up Refrigerator Canyon to Scout Lookout. Many hikers stop here to take in the view. If you're leery of heights and exposed views, don't climb beyond Scout Lookout. Several hikers have fallen to their deaths while ascending the spectacular summit ridge beyond. The last 500 vertical feet between Scout Lookout and Angels Landing is tenuously safeguarded by steel posts and hand chains hikers use to pull themselves up broken sandstone ledges on the exposed ridge line to the flat summit. The perch offers commanding views of Zion Canyon, Kolob Terrace, Cable Mountain, and the Great White Throne. Avoid the summit of Angels Landing during lightning and wind storms when Aeolus, the ancient Greek god, is out in force.

Angels Landing hiker. PHOTO BY NPS

Zion Narrows Riverside Walk and Day Hike

This popular, often crowded 1-mile paved trail leads from the landmark 4,418-foot Temple of Sinawava at the mouth of Zion Canyon to a rest stop at the Zion Narrows crossing. Using walking sticks and trekking poles to balance on the slippery river cobble, many hikers wade and crisscross the Virgin River another 1.6 miles to reach the neck-craning confluence of the 1,000-foot-deep slot of Orderville Canyon entering from the right. Many sandbars along the way offer rest stops to snack, sit, and gaze at the towering Navajo Sandstone cliffs overhead, and shake out the sand and stones from your soggy shoes. (Wading up the Virgin River can be a challenging trek. The water is often painfully cold, and even agile hikers sometimes slip and fall. High water levels may prevent access.)

HIKING ACCESS:

Take the park shuttle to the Riverside Walk Trailhead at the end of Zion Canyon Scenic Drive.

Virgin River flash flood. PHOTO BY NPS

Zion Narrows Canyoneering, Through-Hike

From the Chamberlain Ranch access near the head of the North Fork of the Virgin River at 6,150 feet, this 16-mile canyon route follows the streambed and loses 1,245 vertical feet (76 feet per mile) en route to the Temple of Sinawava at the mouth of Zion Canyon at trail's end. It's possible to through-hike the incredibly beautiful canyon during a single long summer day that begins at first light and ends before sunset. A more leisurely two-day canyon jaunt will include a night out under the stars. Zion Narrows' scenic highlights include seeps, waterfalls, hanging gardens, log jams, and tributary slot canyons that include, from top down, Deep Creek, Kolob Creek, Goose Creek, and Orderville Canyon. Expert canyoneers explore these slots in wetsuits and helmets, using ropes and climbing gear. You can get a paint-by-numbers guide to this rewarding canyon trek, or you can just head down the canyon and take the wonderful surprises and obstacles as they come.

When Major John Wesley Powell and Jacob Hamblin spent two days canyoneering down the neighboring East Fork of the Virgin River in mid-September 1870, Powell described the challenges canyoneers sometimes face: "Wading again this morning; sinking in the quicksand, swimming the deep waters, and making slow and painful progress where the waters are swift, and the bed of the stream rocky." Although such conditions can occur any time of year, it's wise to avoid the Narrows early in the season when spring snowmelt runs high and cold.

HIKING ACCESS:

To through-hike Zion Narrows from top to bottom: You'll need to arrange a ride to the trailhead or leave your own shuttle vehicle at the Zion Canyon Visitor Center so you can collect your car at the trailhead at trip's end. To reach the trailhead, drive 12.3 miles east on Utah Highway 9, the Zion-Mount Carmel Highway, to the Chamberlain Ranch turnoff, turn left, and drive 16.7 miles north on the dirt North Fork Road to the Chamberlain Ranch Trailhead.

For hiking and camping permits, visit:
www.nps.gov/zion/planyourvisit/upload/ZionWG2013.pdf

For ADA accessibility, visit:
www.nps.gov/zion/planyourvisit/accessibility.htm

For more information, visit:
www.nps.gov/zion/index.htm

South Rim Mather Point. PHOTO BY W. TYSON JOYE, NPS

GRAND CANYON NATIONAL PARK

Landscape, People, and Culture

Known as one of The Seven Natural Wonders of the World, the Grand Canyon of the Colorado encompasses 1,904 square miles of the Colorado Plateau in northern Arizona. Seven distinct subplateaus shape its vast topography that stretches west from the Colorado River across the desolate Arizona Strip. All but one are named for the region's indigenous peoples. East to west, Marble Platform, Kaibab, Kanab, Uninkaret, and Shivwits Plateaus form the high country north of the Colorado River, and the Coconino and Hualapai Plateaus form the high country to the south. The canyon's incomparable biodiversity ranges from the 9,241-foot Kaibab Plateau's lush evergreen forests and meadows to the prickly pear cactus-covered benches and alluvial fans of the Colorado River. Coursing and tumbling from Lees Ferry 177 miles to Lake Mead, the Colorado River carved downward through a 1.7-billion-year-old strata of rock layers and unconformities, in places a mile thick, between the Permian-aged Kaibab Limestone of the North and South Rims to the Precambrian-aged Vishnu Schist in the Colorado River corridor. Contributing to the canyon's extraordinary topography, beauty, and inaccessibility are 77 deep, rugged tributary chasms that spill into the granite gorges of the Colorado River.

Eight to 16 miles wide, the Grand Canyon is 6,720 feet deep. Imagine it, if you will, as an inverted mountain range. Geologist Edwin D. McKee put forth this idea when he contributed to the 1948 book, *The Inverted Mountains: Canyons of the West.* A renowned 1930s-era Grand Canyon National Park ranger and naturalist, McKee wrote: "Canyons in the Plateau Country are legion. Some big, some small, they are like the ranges, peaks and foothills of a great mountain system in reverse." Archaic hunters and gatherers, and later Ancestral Puebloans, established a knowledge and affinity for climbing to and building cliff dwellings nestled in the caves and crags of sheer walls in the canyon's inverted mountains. Their intimate knowledge of the canyon's colorful, complex geology enabled them to travel along broken ledges, hanging terraces, and platforms that stretched from one end of the canyon to the other. Carrying food and water in baskets suspended by tump lines on their foreheads, they wore thin hand-woven yucca fiber sandals in order to negotiate daring ascents and descents on foot through sharp, precipitous layers of rock that, taken alone, were up to 500 feet thick. Their faint paths were later traced by the Hopi, Navajo, Yavapai, and Hualapai, and the Kaibab, Uninkaret, and Shivwits bands of Southern Paiutes who viewed the landscape as a sacred home, not an inescapable prison as had outsiders who became lost in the great abyss. Spanish explorers tried following the ancient footpaths that were later improved by prospectors who used the "miner trails" in hopes of

Toroweap Point. PHOTO BY JOHN ANNERINO

Sunset, Grand Canyon. PHOTO BY JOHN ANNERINO

discovering the mother lode. Many of the rugged rim-to-river inner canyon trails still bear the names of miners who used them to carry their picks, shovels, ore, and grub in and out of the canyon on the backs of burros and mules. Among them was the white-bearded Louis D. Boucher, storytelling Captain John Hance, prospector and moonshiner Seth B. Tanner, and pioneer William Wallace Bass leading his burro Joe and burro-riding dog Shep. Their tall tales and steep trails still delight modern visitors and hikers.

All trails led to the Colorado River. As recounted by a Hopi Antelope priest, a young man called *Ti-Yo* hollowed out a cottonwood log and journeyed down the legendary river long before Spanish conquistador García López de Cárdenas first saw the Grand Canyon from the South Rim in September 1540. Prospector and horse thief James White wrote a letter to his brother Josh on September 26, 1867, describing his harrowing adventure through the "Big Cañon" on a rudimentary log raft to escape Indians whose horse he had stolen. During his epic journey, the emaciated White survived by eating dog meat he'd traded for with natives who lived in the canyon. The Hualapai and Paiute, it's been documented, also floated back and forth on logs across the Colorado River to trade and travel. But it wasn't until Major John Wesley Powell journeyed down the "great unknown" in the name of exploration and scientific inquiry that the *Río Colorado*, or "Red River," fired the imagination of all those who followed: surveyors, pioneer photographers, railroad men, geologists, honeymooners, river runners, and adventurers.

Seen from rim or river, the greatest canyon on Earth continues to beckon all comers; 4.5 million American and international visitors hear the siren call each year. Fully 90 percent of them visit the South Rim, leaving the North Rim relatively uncrowded.

Rafting, Grand Canyon. PHOTO BY JOHN ANNERINO

Grand Canyon Lodge interior. PHOTO BY MICHAEL QUINN, NPS

Grand Canyon National Monument was established by President Theodore Roosevelt on January 11, 1908. Now comprising 1,218,375 acres, Grand Canyon National Park was established by President Woodrow Wilson on February 26, 1919. The Grand Canyon is listed as a UNESCO World Heritage Site.

North Rim Highlights

North Rim Campground. Nestled in the ponderosa pines on the edge of a 4,000-foot-deep chasm called the Transept, the North Rim Campground offers 12 tent-only campsites, 3 group sites, and 75 tent/RV sites that include picnic tables, fire grills, and water. Amenities include a general store, pay phones, and pay showers and laundry. The 3-mile round-trip Transept Trail leads from the North Rim Campground to Grand Canyon Lodge.

DRIVING ACCESS:

From Kanab, Utah: Drive 6.4 miles south on U.S. Highway 89A to Fredonia, Arizona. Stay on US 89A and drive south 30.1 miles to Jacob Lake, Arizona. Stop at the Kaibab Plateau Visitor Center to see the environmental display of the flora, fauna, geology, and fire science of the North Rim. It's located next to the historic Jacob Lake Inn. Turn right on paved Arizona Highway 67 and drive 43.4 miles south on the scenic Kaibab Plateau-North Rim Parkway to the parking area at Bright Angel Point in Grand Canyon National Park.

To reach the South Rim, from Flagstaff, Arizona: Drive 50 miles north on U.S. Highway 180 to the junction with Arizona Highway 64. Turn right and drive 29 miles north on U.S. 180/AZ 64 to the Grand Canyon South Rim Visitor Center.

Jacob Lake Fire Lookout. Located 1 mile south of the Kaibab Plateau Visitor Center, stop and visit the Jacob Lake Fire Lookout on the left. Built by the Civilian Conservation Corps in 1934, the 80-foot steel tower was originally named the Bright Angel Point Fire Lookout, but was relocated and renamed Jacob Lake Fire Lookout. It's listed on the National Register of Historic Places. Author and environmentalist Edward Abbey spent four seasons in the tower where he wrote his 1971 novel, *Black Sun*, about a fire lookout. From the steel room with a view atop the tower, you can see the Kaibab Plateau's forests of Engelmann and blue spruce, aspen, and ponderosa pine, and the devastation wrought by the 2006 Warm Fire, which burned 58,640 acres on the crest of the Kaibab Plateau.

Bright Angel Point. From the visitor center, you can follow the paved 0.5-mile path to 8,255-foot Bright Angel Point for a sunrise or sunset view of the inner canyon. Or you can take in the view from the spectacular limestone balcony of the Grand Canyon Lodge. Across the canyon you can easily see the volcanic pyramid of 12,633-foot Humphrey's Peak in the San Francisco Mountains, which are revered by the Grand Canyon's native peoples. Their Hopi name is *Nuvatekiaqui*, or "Place of Snow on the Very Top," the Navajo name is *Dook'o'oslííd*, or "Never Thaws on Top," and the Havasupai name is *Hvehasahpatch*, or "Big Rock Mountain." Closer at hand you can study three spectacular landmark spires that were named by geologist Clarence E. Dutton in 1882. Left to right they include 7,363-foot Deva Temple, 7,651-foot Brahma Temple, and 7,125-foot Zoroaster Temple. Each of the precarious summits have been climbed, offering climbers a canyon adventure like no other and views of the deep abyss described by Dutton as "one of the finest and perhaps the most picturesque of gorges in the whole Kaibab front."

North Kaibab Trail Day Hike and Trek.

Used by Ancestral Puebloans as a seasonal access route through Bright Angel Canyon from the North Rim to the Colorado River, Major John Wesley Powell named it Bright Angel Canyon on August 18 during his 1869 Colorado River expedition to find "timber from which to make oars." The expedition search was limited to the Bright Angel Creek area. But 22 years later, New York-born, Flagstaff, Arizona, resident Daniel L. Hogan and his partner Henry Ward made the first recorded ascent and descent of the rugged canyon—and the first rim-to-rim crossing of the Grand Canyon—while prospecting for copper in 1891. Little is known of the pair's canyon crossing, but Hogan later served in the 1st United States

North Kaibab Trail. PHOTO BY NPS

Volunteer Cavalry under Colonel Theodore Roosevelt with his Roughriders during the Spanish American War in Cuba in 1898. With seemingly little fear of heights, Hogan discovered and filed the Orphan Lode Mining Claim on March 23, 1906, for a glory hole in the cliff walls 1,800 feet below the South Rim that President Theodore Roosevelt authorized. U.S. Geological Survey cartographer François Matthes and his party forged a rough trail down the canyon in the winter of 1902, fording Bright Angel Creek 94 times while surveying for the Grand Canyon's first topographical map. The original 18-mile-long route descended Bright Angel Canyon, and Matthes reported, "So steep was it that the animals [horses and mules] fairly slid down on their haunches." The Dutch-born cartographer's resulting Bright Angel Quadrangle was considered "topographic art," and it opened the doors for artists, geologists, photographers, hikers, mule skinners, canyoneers, and rim-to-rim runners.

A rim-to-river hike in the Grand Canyon can be difficult for many hikers under the best of circumstances. It's easy to be pulled by gravity into the canyon, but far more difficult to climb out. The 14.2-mile-long North Kaibab Trail loses 5,816 vertical feet in its descent to the Colorado River, and gains 5,816 vertical feet on the ascent. If you're not acclimated to the high altitude, or healthy and fit from cardiovascular exercise, first try hiking the 1.5-mile rim-top Transept Trail accessed at the North Rim Campground. Or limit your North Kaibab Trail hike to the 1.4-mile round-trip hike to the Coconino Overlook. It's strongly advised not to descend farther than Roaring Springs for a day hike. Backpackers must stay at designated campsites: Cottonwood Campground at the halfway point, and Bright Angel Campground near Phantom Ranch. The upper trail is often icy and snowbound in winter. The hiking season typically runs from mid-May to mid-October. Below are the mileages and elevation points for scenic stops and destinations along the North Kaibab Trail.

- 0.7 mile, Coconino Overlook.
- 1.7 miles, Supai Tunnel, 6,800 feet. Potable water available.
- 4.7 miles, Roaring Springs, 5,220 feet. Potable water available. **Day Hike Turnaround!** (Short side hike to Roaring Springs and Pump House.) Potable water available at Pump House residence.
- 6.9 miles, Cottonwood Campground, 4,080 feet. Potable water available.
- 8.4 miles, Ribbon Falls, 3,720 feet. (Short side hike to Ribbon Falls.)
- 14 miles, Phantom Ranch and Bright Angel Campground, 2,480 feet. Potable water available.
- 14.2 miles, Colorado River, 2,425 feet.

HIKING ACCESS:

From the North Rim Campground: Walk or drive 0.5 mile to the North Kaibab Trailhead and parking lot, at 8,241 feet.

Shiva Temple, North Rim. PHOTO BY JOHN ANNERINO

South Rim Highlights

The South Rim is busiest from May through September, so if possible, plan your trip for a quieter season. In December and January, scenic overlooks are accessible by private vehicle. To sample the scenic overlooks from March through November, park in one of the four large lots surrounding the South Rim Visitor Center and then board one of the park's free shuttle buses. The Kaibab/Rim and Hermit Road Routes cover scenic overlooks east and west, respectively, from the South Rim Visitor Center. The Hiker's Express Shuttle provides service to the South Kaibab Trailhead. The Village Route does not stop at scenic overlooks but provides access to lodging, Mather Campground, shopping, and the visitor center.

South Kaibab Trail Day Hike. The South Kaibab Trail offers the best views for a short day hike below the rim. The trail begins south of Yaki Point on Yaki Point Road at an elevation of 7,260 feet. There is no water below the rim and very

South Rim sunset. PHOTO BY MICHAEL QUINN, NPS

little shade. Carry plenty of drinking water, and plan on your uphill return to take twice as long as the walk down. Hike 0.9 mile (and 600 feet downhill) to Ooh-Aah Point for broad, spectacular views. For a longer hike, continue down another 0.6 mile (and 540 feet) to Cedar Ridge, which offers good views and restrooms. Do not hike past Cedar Ridge in hot weather. Allow plenty of daylight to hike the 1.5 miles and 1,140 feet back to the rim.

Yavapai Museum of Geology. The Grand Canyon's geology is so vast—over time and space—it can be overwhelming. Perched at canyon's edge, this museum's excellent exhibits and three-dimensional models bring big ideas down to scale, showing the chronology of rock deposition, Colorado Plateau uplift, and the cutting action of the river. The museum is 0.7 mile west of the South Rim Visitor Center, accessible either by the South Entrance Road or the Rim Trail.

For further information, visit: www.nps.gov/grca/index.htm

South Rim, Bright Angel Trail. PHOTO BY MICHAEL QUINN, NPS

SUGGESTED READING

Abbey, Edward. *Desert Solitaire: A Season in the Wilderness.* New York: Ballantine Books, 1968.

___. *Slickrock: Endangered Canyons of the Southwest* (photographs and commentary by Philip Hyde). New York: Sierra Club/Charles Scribner's Sons, 1971.

Annerino, John. *Indian Country: Sacred Ground, Native People* (photography by the author). New York: W. W. Norton & Company, 2007.

Bolton, Herbert E. *Pageant in the Wilderness: The Story of the Escalante Expedition to the Interior Basin, 1776, Including the Diary and Itinerary of Father Escalante, Translated and Annotated.* Salt Lake City: Utah Historical Society, 1950.

Crampton, C. Gregory. *Standing Up Country: The Canyon Lands of Utah and Arizona.* New York and Salt Lake City: Alfred A. Knopf and University of Utah Press in association with the Amon Carter Museum of Western Art, 1964.

Dellenbaugh, Frederick S. *A Canyon Voyage: The Narrative of the Second Powell Expedition Down the Green-Colorado River from Wyoming, and the Explorations on Land, in the Years 1871 and 1872.* New York and London: G.P. Putnam's Sons, 1908.

Dutton, Clarence E. *Report on the Geology of the High Plateaus of Utah, with Atlas.* U.S. Geographical and Geological Survey of the Rocky Mountain Region. Washington, DC: Government Printing Office, 1880.

Gregory, Herbert E., and Robert C. Moore. *The Kaiparowits Region: A Geographic and Geologic Reconnaissance of Utah and Arizona.* U.S. Department of the Interior Professional Paper 164. Washington, DC: U.S. Government Printing Office, 1931.

Grey, Zane. *Tales of Lonely Trails.* New York and London: Harper & Brothers, 1922., 1986.

Horan, James D. *Desperate Men: The James Gang and the Wild Bunch.* New York, Doubleday, 1949.

Lee, John D. A *Mormon Chronicle, The Diaries of John D. Lee, 1848-1876* (edited and annotated by Robert Glass Cleland and Juanita Brooks). San Marino, CA: Huntington Library, 1955.

Lee, Katie. *All My Rivers Are Gone.* Boulder, CO: Johnson Books, 1998.

Linford, Laurance D. *Navajo Places: History, Legend, Landscape.* Salt Lake City: University of Utah Press, 2000.

Luckert, Karl W. *Navajo Mountain and Rainbow Bridge Religion.* Flagstaff, AZ: Museum of Northern Arizona, 1977.

Nichols, Tad. *Glen Canyon: Images of a Lost World* (photographs by the author). Santa Fe: Museum of New Mexico Press, 1999.

Peattie, Roderick, editor. *The Inverted Mountains: Canyons of the West* (contributors Harold S. Colton, Weldon F. Heald, Edwin D. McKee). New York: Vanguard Press, 1948.

Porter, Eliot. *The Place No One Knew: Glen Canyon on the Colorado* (edited by David Brower). San Francisco: Sierra Club Books, 1963.

Powell, J. W. *Exploration of the Colorado River of the West and Its Tributaries. Explored in 1869, 1870, 1871, and 1872, Under the Direction of the Secretary of the Smithsonian Institution.* Washington, DC: Government Printing Office, 1875.

Reisner, Marc. *Cadillac Desert: The American West and Its Disappearing Water.* New York: Penguin Books, 1986.

Ruess, Everett. *On Desert Trails with Everett Ruess,* El Centro, CA: Desert Magazine Press, 1940.

Thompson, A. H. "Report on a Trip to the Mouth of the Dirty Devil River" in *Exploration of the Colorado River of the West and Its Tributaries. Explored in 1869, 1870, 1871, and 1872* by J. W. Powell. Washington, DC: Government Printing Office, 1875.

INDEX

Bold face numbers indicate photographs.

ABOUT THE AUTHOR

John Annerino's adventure and landscape photography, features, and writing have been published in many magazines including *Arizona Highways, LIFE, National Geographic Adventure, Outdoor Photography, UK,* and *Travel & Leisure,* and also books and calendars published by Sierra Club Books and W. W. Norton. John has worked as a heli-tac forest fire crew boss in Alaska and the West, a whitewater boatman on the Green, Yampa, Upper Salt, and Colorado Rivers, and as a wilderness guide and outdoor educator in the Grand Canyon, Arizona, and in Mexico.